To Broc
&
Mac

[signature] 89

Go Wor Eagles!!

Praise for *A Better Man*

"It's one thing to tell [someone] how to act and another thing entirely to show him. *A Better Man* does the latter through poignant stories about real people, told by the very people who lived them. This book provides lessons that pave the way to a newer, brighter future for men who will not only achieve great things in their lives, but also in the lives of the better men they will raise and mentor. Thank you, Kelly Johnson, for giving parents, educators and young people a book that will positively influence the lives of our nation's men for generations to come."

—Michael Gurian, Author of *The Wonder of Boys* and *The Purpose of Boys*

"We are a nation in constant motion toward fulfilling the aspiration of equality. The life lessons from these amazing men are a true gift to the next generation of young people of all races, all nationalities, all walks of life. Kelly Johnson has compiled a treasure trove of honest and intimate experiences that will open eyes and hearts . . . and inspire anyone who reads it—man, woman, parent, or child—to take bold steps to better themselves and the world."

—Doug Shipman, Executive Director, Center for Civil and Human Rights

"*A Better Man* is a splendid compilation of interviews and essays of men who are role models for all of us. [It] could well make a difference in the lives of young males . . . facing the challenges of manhood. Also, I am confident young women would be motivated and inspired by the great stories of the distinguished men whose experiences could be defined as appropriate for feminine growth and development."

—Frances Bartlett Kinne, Ph.D., Chancellor Emeritus and Past President Jacksonville University, Jacksonville, Florida

"It is my honor to recommend the book *A Better Man*; its author, Kelly Johnson; and any program that introduces the book to young men and women. *A Better Man* is teeming with relevant, inspiring life lessons for our youth today. [The] amazing men in the book make a powerful impact and bring these lessons to life."

—Elizabeth K. Armbruster, Principal, Mills E. Godwin High School, Henrico, Virginia

"There is a disquieting trend in our society towards accepting less than our best—and it's bled over into the outlook we have for the boys we are raising into men. *A Better Man* reminds us not to settle but to encourage our sons, our nephews, our brothers, and our neighbors to cultivate within themselves those qualities that make them better men: men of drive, honor, compassion, and integrity. Every young man would greatly benefit from the lessons learned in this book. Its positive impact will be felt for generations to come."

   —Ambassador Andrew J. Young, Jr.

"I believe this book, *A Better Man*, has the potential to have a powerful impact . . . . The selection of men interviewed is itself so diverse in age, occupation, and ethnicity that the appeal is very broad. [It] is a powerful volume for our youth."

   —George F. Towery, Principal, Cameron Elementary School, Alexandria, Virginia

"Kelly Johnson has brought together twenty-six true American heroes and asked them to share some of their thoughts and insights on a host of topics. The result is a book of timeless wisdom that offers [a] unique opportunity to hear from great men their stories, the lessons they've learned, and the truth about being a man. It is a book whose time has come."

   —Captain Robert C. Hurd, USN (Ret.), Congressional Liaison, U.S. Naval Sea Cadet Corps

"I recommend [*A Better Man*] highly to all high schools, not only for males but for females alike. The important message it sends cannot be matched by any other I have encountered. Thank you so much Kelly Harrington Johnson! Well done!"

   —Shannon Poole Grable, Counselor, North Brunswick High School, North Carolina

"I asked my [7th grade] students if they would write their thoughts about the book and its message. Here are a few of their comments: 'This book is inspiring to not just boys but girls too! *A Better Man* is a wonderful book!' . . . 'It changes your perspective on some things and makes you think of how you've been living your life . . . and it also says that even though you're ordinary you can do extraordinary things.' . . . This book lifts the reader up and makes us believe in the power we each hold within."

   —Diana Barron, 7th Grade Teacher, Richmond, Virginia

"[*A Better Man*] is an inspiring collection of essays and interviews . . . . I also believe that this book can be a help to some who are given the opportunity to create a better life after having gone the wrong direction. For that reason, I have recommended that copies of *A Better Man* be purchased for our court for use in a new re-entry program . . . designed to have judges and others work directly with small numbers of federal prisoners upon their entry into post-prison supervised release."

—Judge W. Harold Albritton, Senior United States District Judge, Montgomery, Alabama

"As a Navy chaplain for thirty-three years and a former Chief of Chaplains the last three of those years, I have spent considerable time with young sailors and marines . . . [A]ll too often it is apparent that there was no guiding hand during their formative years. Using their own experiences, and with a desire to be a positive influence for many who, until now, have been neglected, these heroes [in *A Better Man*] tell life stories and share positive values with a love and admiration for our nation's young men."

—Rear Admiral Byron Holderby, Chaplain, United States Navy (Ret.)

A Better Man

A Better Man

True American Heroes Speak to Young Men *and Women*
on Love, Power, Pride and What It *Really* Means to Be a Man

Edited by Kelly H. Johnson

Warmest regards,

Kelly H. Johnson

❈ *Brandylane*

Copyright 2009, 2015 by Kelly H. Johnson. First edition, 2009. Second edition, 2015.
All rights reserved under international and Pan-American Copyright conventions. No portion of this book may be reproduced in any form or medium whatsoever without the written permission of the publisher.

Civility © 2009 by Harry L. Carrico
Choices © 2009 by Fred K. Bruney
Fail! © 2009 by Dee Bradley Baker
Hard-Headed © 2009 by Tim Seibles
Killing the Spider © 2009 by Kevin Smith
The Mediocrity Trap © 2009 by L. Douglas Wilder
No Such Thing as a Bad Day © 2009 by Paul E. Galanti
To Forgive © 2009 by Kenny Leon
On a Positive Note © 2009 by Roger A. Schmitz
Character, Integrity and Perseverance © 2009 by Howard Petrea
Uncommon Courage © 2009 by John W. Ripley
Whose Life Is It Anyway? © 2009 by Leighton W. Smith, Jr.

All interviews are jointly copyrighted 2009 by Kelly H. Johnson and interviewee.

COVER PHOTOS
(Pictured from left to right)
Top Row: Dominique Wilkins, Ambassador Andrew J. Young, Jr., Adam Cristman, Kenny Leon
Second Row: Col. John W. Ripley and friend, Tavis Smiley, Tim Seibles, Comdr. Paul E. Galanti
Third Row: Matt Hasselbeck, Adm. Leighton W. Smith, Jr., Tim Reid, The Honorable Harry L. Carrico
Bottom Row: President George Herbert Walker Bush, The Honorable L. Douglas Wilder, Col. John W. Ripley, Ray Allen

Photo Copyrights:
Photo of Ray Allen appears courtesy NBA Photos; photo of President George Herbert Walker Bush appears courtesy Alexander's/Houston; photo of Senior Justice Harry L. Carrico appears courtesy Tom Trenz; photo of Adam Cristman appears courtesy Keith Nordstrom/New England Revolution; photo of Comdr. Paul E. Galanti appears courtesy Time Inc.; photo of Matt Hasselbeck appears courtesy Seattle Seahawks; photo of Will Heller appears courtesy Corky Trewin/Seattle Seahawks; photo of Tim Reid appears courtesy Tim and Daphne Reid/New Millennium Studios; photo of Col. John W. Ripley and friend appears courtesy the Ripley family; portrait of Col. John W. Ripley is taken from "THE MARINES," copyright Anthony Edgeworth; photo of Tim Seibles appears courtesy Chuck Thomas; photo of Tavis Smiley appears courtesy Kevin Foley; photo of the Honorable L. Douglas Wilder appears courtesy the Library of Virginia; photo of Dominique Wilkins appears courtesy NBA Photos; photo of Ambassador Andrew J. Young, Jr. appears courtesy Spider Martin (1965 Spider Martin. All rights reserved. Used with permission).

Jacket design by Tom Trenz of Brandylane Publishers, Inc.; and Fred Johnson

Printed in the United States of America

ISBN 978-1-9399302-6-2
Library of Congress Control Number: 2014942393

Brandylane
Richmond, Virginia
brandylanepublishers.com

For the girls—who saw that the book was relevant to their lives right from the start and, with courage and courtesy, always made a point of telling me so. I am forever in your debt.

And, as before, to Phillip H. Harrington, the man I am immensely proud to call my father. He has believed in me since the day I was born; and this book, like so many other things in my life, would not have been possible without him.

Table of Contents

Acknowledgments xvi

A Special Note Regarding this Edition xx

The Greater Good xxiii
An Introduction by Kelly Johnson
Featuring former President George Herbert Walker Bush

1. **Ambassador Andrew J. Young, Jr.** 1
   Topic: Higher purpose

2. **Admiral Leighton W. Smith, Jr., USN (Ret.)** 11
   Whose Life Is It Anyway?
   Topic: Responsibility

3. **Tim Seibles** 23
   Hard-Headed
   Topics: Dreams; goals

4. **Ray Allen** 33
   Topics: Respect for women; success; general advice

5. **Colonel John W. Ripley, USMC** 45
   Uncommon Courage
   Topic: Courage in daily life

6. **Kenny Leon** 55
   To Forgive
   Topic: Forgiveness

7. **Father Hector LaChapelle** 63
   Topic: Faith

8. **Commander Paul E. Galanti, USN (Ret.)** 73
   No Such Thing as a Bad Day
   Topic: Overcoming hardship

9. **Tim Reid** 83
   Topics: Media influence; role models; general advice

10. **Matt Hasselbeck** 95
    Topics: Leadership; integrity

11. **Kevin Smith** 105
    Killing the Spider
    Topic: Anger

12. **Adam Cristman** 117
    Topics: Respect for women; media influence; general advice

13. **Dee Bradley Baker** 129
    Fail!
    Topics: Risks; failure

14. **Dominique Wilkins** 137
    Topics: Bullying; self-respect; general advice

15. **The Honorable L. Douglas Wilder** 151
    The Mediocrity Trap
    Topics: Excellence; opportunity

16. **Major General Ronald L. Johnson, USA (Ret.)** 161
    Topics: Choices; consequences; redemption

17. **Will Heller** 171
    Topics: Persistence; humility

18. **Michael Bantom** 183
    Topics: Faith; success; general advice

19. **The Honorable Harry L. Carrico** 195
    Civility
    Topic: Civility

20. **Tavis Smiley** 205
    Topics: Profanity; media influence

21. **Professor Roger A. Schmitz, Ph.D.** 215
    On a Positive Note
    Topics: Attitudes; outlook

22. **Kevin Willis** 221
    Topics: Violence; tolerance; general advice

23. **Captain Howard "Rusty" Petrea, USN (Ret.)** 233
    Character, Integrity and Perseverance
    Topics: Character; integrity; perseverance

24. **Fred K. Bruney** 243
    Choices
    Topic: Choice; consequence

25. **Christopher E. Tubbs, Ph.D.** 251
    Topics: Being true to oneself; general advice

Contributing Authors
(by area of expertise)

I. Politicians/Government Officials/Activists

1. George Herbert Walker Bush,
    former president of the United States xxiii
2. Harry L. Carrico, senior justice, Supreme Court of Virginia ... 195
3. Tavis Smiley, radio and television commentator 205
4. L. Douglas Wilder, former governor of Virginia,
    Civil Rights activist....................................... 151
5. Andrew J. Young, Jr., Civil Rights icon...................... 1

II. Military

1. Comdr. Paul E. Galanti, USN (Ret.) 73
2. Maj. Gen. Ronald L. Johnson, USA (Ret.). 161
3. Capt. Howard "Rusty" Petrea, USN (Ret.) 233
4. Col. John W. Ripley, USMC 45
5. Adm. Leighton W. Smith, Jr., USN (Ret.). 11

III. Professional Sports

1. Ray Allen, NBA 33
2. Michael Bantom, NBA 183
3. Fred Bruney, NFL 243
4. Adam Cristman, MLS....................................... 117
5. Matt Hasselbeck, NFL 95
6. Will Heller, NFL. 171
7. Ronald L. Johnson, NBA 161
8. Kevin Willis, NBA 221
9. Dominique Wilkins, NBA................................... 137

IV. Academicians

1. Roger A. Schmitz, Ph.D., University of Notre Dame. 215
2. Tim Seibles, Old Dominion University 23
3. Kevin Smith, youth counselor, San Diego, California 105
4. Christopher E. Tubbs, Ph.D., Vertex Pharmaceuticals. 251

V. Arts/Entertainment

1. Dee Bradley Baker, Hollywood voice artist 129
2. Kenny Leon, Broadway and film director. 55
3. Tim Reid, actor/director/producer. 83
4. Tim Seibles, poet. 23
5. Tavis Smiley, television and radio commentator. 205

VI. Clergy/Philanthropists

1. Father Hector LaChapelle, Roman Catholic priest 63
2. Howard "Rusty" Petrea, co-founder,
     The First Tee of Brunswick County. 233

Acknowledgments

When I think of the number of people to whom I owe a debt of gratitude for helping bring this book to fruition, I am overwhelmed both by their numbers and by the magnitude of all that they have done for me. And while there can be no true order of thanks for all the help and kindness shown to me throughout this process, it is only fitting that I begin at the beginning. Thus, thanks go first and foremost to the five young men whose existence gave birth to this book, my boys—Cole, Connor, Phil, Daelan and Parker. I am so very proud of each of you. Thanks go next to my baby girl, Ellery, who greets life with a joy and optimism that never ceases to amaze me. I extend a very special thank you to my beloved husband, Fred, whose sacrifices on our behalf are nearly superhuman. I love you.

Thanks go next to my dad, to whom this book is dedicated and whose name should rightfully be on the cover with mine. He was my silent co-editor from start to finish and I am indebted to him in ways impossible to describe. I owe deep thanks also to my mother, Reggie Harrington. I came into this world such a fragile, frightened little being and, more than anything else, it was her mothering that saved me. I can't imagine my life without her gentle, guiding presence.

Elizabeth Austen, Lisa Kelly and Leslie Sadler have supported me through all the ups and downs in the way that only best friends can. I owe each of you so very much. I am indebted too to Joe Wood, Jeannie Kuhnert, Leigh Kineston, Karen Meardon and Lindsey Piett for always making the impossible feel like it was within reach. Of course, this list wouldn't be complete without a big shout-out to Heidi Abbott, Betty Blondeau-Russell, Emerson Bruns, Chrysa Chin, Anthony Edgeworth, Brandon Ford, Mary McGee, Tat Perrill, Joni Schmitz, Kristen Schremp and Terrell Slayton.

Acknowledgments

I will always be grateful to Kimberly McFarland, Linda Poepsel, Lindsay Robinson, Ruth Jones and Ryan Mullins for the graciousness and patience they showed me each and every time I called or sent *yet another* e-mail. Admiral Chris Paul, I hope you'll let me buy you that cup of coffee. Tracy Martin, I'm so proud to have your dad's photo on the cover of this book.

Most authors can only dream of being the beneficiary of the kind of talent and excellence my "team" of publicists brought to the table: Jenny Costantino, who deserves her very own category; Heather Prestwood, who keeps me both sane and organized (no small feat); and Dottie DeHart, who steered the train and made it all happen.

Few men were as critical to this endeavor as Robert Pruett, my publisher, who is the best in the business in every conceivable way.

Steve Kelley would kill me if I blew his cover and told you what a wonderfully kind human being he is, so I'll just thank him for his friendship and his faith in me (and for drying my tears the first day we met). There aren't enough pages in this book for all of the "thank yous" I owe to my dear friend Daphne Reid, so I'll just thank her for *everything*. I am indebted too to Melinda and Randy Edwards, who went to bat for me more than once and hit it out of the park, and to Capt. Dick Stratton for allowing me to use his terrific story about the day he met "Boat School Boy," Paul Galanti. Finally, a special thanks is owed to my Uncle Terry, who pieced me back together during one of my darkest hours.

Last, but certainly not least, are the men whose words and wisdom fill these pages. Though I will address them largely in alphabetical order, I must begin with the man who first signed on to this adventure, Senior Justice Harry L. Carrico. With no other gentlemen yet on board, he agreed to write for the book based solely on his faith in me. It was a profound vote of confidence that carried me through many of the challenges that followed. I will never, ever forget it.

I extend heartfelt thanks:

to Ray Allen, who agreed to jump in at the last minute and then gave such a powerful and heartfelt interview;

to Dee Baker, who found a way to write an essay that manages to be deeply funny and deeply wise;

to Mike Bantom, who had to endure my first interview—the one before I got the kinks out;

to Fred Bruney, who sat patiently through my first "presentation," which, if memory serves, lasted over an hour;

to former President George Herbert Walker Bush, whose participation honors me beyond description;

to Adam Cristman, who gave a remarkable interview that reinvigorated my faith in young men;

to Matt Hasselbeck, who agreed to go through with the interview despite the fact that we had to conduct it on plastic chairs, in a hallway, beside an elevator;

to Will Heller, because he never gave up and because he is too humble to see how truly incredible that is;

to Maj. Gen. Ron Johnson, because I will forever consider our meeting one of the great personal blessings of this book;

to Father Hector LaChapelle, for shedding light on the most important path of all;

to Kenny Leon, who never once put me on hold because someone famous was on the other line—a remarkable lesson in decency;

to Rusty Petrea, whose vision and commitment to "walking the walk" are a constant source of inspiration;

to Tim Reid, for his time, wisdom and friendship;

to Roger Schmitz, to whom I still owe the "full story";

to Tim Seibles, for an essay that reads like poetry in both its cadence and its honesty;

to Tavis Smiley, for telling it like it is;

to Kevin Smith, who healed his pain, moved on with his life, and then had the courage to come back and teach others to do the same;

to Chris Tubbs, who lived on both sides of that greener grass and decided to grow his own damn lawn;

to Mayor Wilder, who took a leap of faith based on one meeting;

to Dominique Wilkins, who lived up to the hype;

to Kevin Willis, whose friendship has been an unexpected and wonderful blessing; and

to Ambassador Andrew Young, who let me tag along with him for a day, gave me an incredible interview, and then showered me with gifts before I left.

Last, I extend deepest thanks to the men I call the "Magnificent Three": Adm. Leighton W. Smith, Jr., Comdr. Paul E. Galanti, and Col. John W. Ripley —classmates of my father's at the United States Naval Academy.

Acknowledgments

They each received a call or an e-mail from my dad, virtually out of the blue, asking if they would consider writing an essay "for a book [his] daughter was writing." Without any hesitation, all three of them said that they would. Not only did they provide three incredible essays, but they became my most stalwart supporters, encouraging me when I felt down, ordering me to buck-up if I tried to complain, and threatening to "kick down doors" for me as needed. They had more faith in me than I ever could have had in myself, and I owe them a debt I will be hard-pressed to repay. They each hold a piece of my heart, and I will count them among my friends to the end of my days.

A Special Note Regarding this Edition

Much has changed since the first edition of this book was published. Some of these changes are pretty fantastic—like Kenny Leon winning a Tony Award for *A Raisin in the Sun*; Tim Seibles' book, *Fast Animal*, being named one of five finalists for the National Book Award for Poetry; and, Ray Allen adding another NBA Championship title (plus a new shooting record) to his résumé. But other changes, most notably the deaths of Justice Harry L. Carrico and Professor Roger A. Schmitz, left us feeling a little worse for wear.

In between the highs and the lows, of course, a host of other changes have taken place in the lives of the twenty-six men who grace these pages. To fully acknowledge all that has transpired would require and, in fact, *deserves* more than this simple edition can offer. That task is for another day.

Until then, I am comforted knowing that the true significance and power of this book does not reside in the facts of each man's life, but in the *wisdom, insight* and *advice* that follows. And like everything that is most real, these things endure, undiminished by the passage of time.

So why are we here? Why a new edition? The answer lies in the two questions that I have been asked time and time again since *A Better Man* was published. The first question is whether this book has anything to offer girls. The second question is whether I plan to write a book for young women. I've been fascinated at how consistently both questions come up and also by the fact that, while technically distinct, in many ways they are two sides of the same coin.

As to the first question, my answer is always a resounding, "Yes!" The fact is that most of the advice in this book is gender-neutral. After all, when these men talk about things like compassion, faith, integrity and moral courage, they are speaking to the reader's *humanity*, not their gender.

As to the question of when I plan to write a book for girls—finding the right answer is usually more elusive. Strange as it sounds, the most truthful response I can give is that I already have. Or at least, I hope that I have. For several years now, I've watched my daughter and her friends try to find their way in a world that seeks to define them—and their worth—in largely physical and almost always superficial terms. Like most girls their age, they are having to grapple with enormous challenges posed by social media, cultural expectation, and all the other red herrings of self-image facing young women today. So, while it is true that I wrote A Better Man "for" boys, I did not write it *solely* for them. I also wrote it for the sake of all the young women their lives would touch.

More to the point, I wrote *A Better Man* because I hoped that young women would stumble across this book. And when they did, I wanted them to hear what good men had to say about relationships, about the respect men owe to women, about fatherhood, compassion, faith, integrity, and the like. I wanted them to know, beyond any shadow of doubt, that *very* good men of compassion, courage, humor and intelligence really do exist. But most of all, I wanted them to know that when it comes to the men in their lives—when it comes to choosing boyfriends, husbands and even their male friends, they have the right to *set the bar high.*

I dreamed that this message might somehow find its way to them. I dreamed and I hoped. And, it turns out, I completely underestimated how savvy our girls really are. I know this to be the case because I've had the honor of being asked to speak at numerous high schools and youth organizations, sometimes by myself and other times with a few of the men from the book. To my utter delight and astonishment, at every event, there have been girls who have taken the time to come tell me how much certain chapters have meant to them and why. They've shared funny stories and private ones, and recounted moments of insight, both large and small, that they've gleaned from these pages. I recall one young lady telling me flat out, "Mrs. Johnson, I don't mean to be rude, but I wanted to let you know that your book isn't just for boys!" And I will never forget the determined young woman who bought an extra copy for her best friend "because she always settles for boys who treat her bad." She was going to make her friend read it, "so she can see she deserves better."

Last spring, I worked with a group of high school students over the course of several weeks as they prepared to host four of the men from the book at their school. When the big day arrived, they did a fabulous job; and afterward, we celebrated their hard work. As the festivities wound down, I started gathering my things to leave when a few of the girls approached me. Because we'd spent a good deal of time planning for this event, we had already talked about the book's gender-neutral advice and explored the unique insights it offers to girls in particular. In other words, I assumed they were coming over to say good-bye. Instead, they looked me in the eye and told me that they had talked, and that they all agreed I needed to find some way to let girls know that this book was for them too. "Maybe put it on the cover or something," they suggested. "It's important."

Indeed.

And so, here it is, with my deep gratitude to them and to every young woman who took time to tell me what the book meant to her or how it changed her life for the better. In doing so, you made my secret hopes and dreams for this book come true; and, together, you brought this edition to life.

Kelly H. Johnson
June 2014

The Greater Good

An Introduction by Kelly H. Johnson,
featuring former President George Herbert Walker Bush

In 1992, then-President George Herbert Walker Bush and then-Arkansas Governor Bill Clinton were the respective Republican and Democratic nominees for President of the United States. The campaign was difficult and, at times, acrimonious. Attacks from both sides became increasingly personal over the course of the campaign, and the candidates were sharply divided over the ways in which the country should move forward in the coming four years. In the end, President Clinton prevailed, and President Bush was forced to relinquish the presidency after only one term.

Twelve years later, in December 2004, a tsunami slammed the coast of southern Asia, killing hundreds of thousands of people and obliterating coastal communities from India to Indonesia. As nations around the world raced to respond, these two former rivals stepped to the forefront and publicly joined forces in an attempt to galvanize relief efforts for the victims.

Their partnership was met with both suspicion and praise; but in the end, the Bush-Clinton Tsunami Fund proved to be an enormous success. Yet, precisely because it was so successful, it is more difficult, I think, to appreciate what an enormous risk their collaboration was at the start. In fact, both men were warned by trusted advisors of the potential backlash that might result from their partnership; yet they chose to move forward, putting their reputations on the line for what they felt was morally right.

Today, these two men, once so famous for their opposing points of view and fierce fight for the presidency, are friends. Although you can still find critics who claim that the relationship is purely one of convenience, if we are to believe the men themselves, the respect and admiration they feel for one another is genuine. Despite their painful past and disparate political viewpoints, they are both men of compassion, good humor and action, and these shared qualities more than make up for whatever differences remain between them.

Five years after the creation of the Bush-Clinton Tsunami Fund, another American president would embrace this same ideal. In 2009, the country watched as President Barack H. Obama created a bipartisan cabinet, the likes of which had not been seen since President Lincoln's "Team of Rivals."* It was an inspirational and historic moment; yet, personally, I remained intrigued by the Bush/Clinton partnership, and especially by President Bush's willingness to enter into it. After all, as President Clinton himself pointed out in an interview with *Time* magazine, "because [President] Bush had to reconcile with someone who had beaten him, he merited the most praise for making the partnership work."**

I wrote to President Bush and asked if he would provide me with his thoughts on his collaboration with President Clinton. Specifically, I wondered what lesson he hoped readers might take away from their example. He kindly took time from his schedule to respond and has allowed me to reprint the following:

> *When in life you find yourself on opposite sides of an issue from another person or group of persons, I encourage you to engage in the kind of rigorous debate upon which our great country is founded. However, I hope also that you will be mindful never to let those differences become a chasm which you cannot cross for the sake of a greater good. Indeed, "a better man" is one who understands that he can put aside differences without surrendering his beliefs.*
>
> *President Clinton and I tried to put this principle into practice in the wake of two natural disasters. The image*

---

*"Team of Rivals" refers both to the bipartisan cabinet appointed by Abraham Lincoln when he became president in 1860, and to the title of a book written by renowned presidential historian, Doris Kearns Goodwin. *Team of Rivals: The Political Genius of Abraham Lincoln* (New York: Simon & Schuster, 2005).

**Michael Duffy, "When Opposites Attract," Time, (December 19, 2005), http://www.time.com/time/magazine/article/09171,1142266,00.html.

> *of two former political adversaries working together on two humanitarian causes–the Bush-Clinton Tsunami Fund and the Bush-Clinton Katrina Fund–has resonated around the world. I have been told by a number of friends abroad that this is something that would not happen in many other countries.*
>
> *It was an honor working with President Clinton on these two projects. I believe it has sent a message for others that it is possible and essential to set aside political differences in the interest of humankind.*

Plainly, President Bush's decision to enter into this partnership was not prompted by political interests, but by a fierce determination to pursue a course of action he felt had the greatest chance of helping the most people. The same, of course, can be said of President Clinton. Their hope that a collaborative effort would increase the effectiveness of the relief efforts to the tsunami victims vastly outweighed whatever personal or political risk that came with it.

Most of us will never have the opportunity to act on a global scale as these two gentlemen did; but that does not mean that their example is less relevant to our lives. In fact, in some ways what is asked of us is even more daunting because, more often than not, we must choose to act nobly without any reasonable expectation of receiving credit for doing so. I know for myself, I'm willing to work side by side with almost anyone if the cause is important–or glamorous–enough. But when it comes to the mundane stuff–where, for example, I'm asked to work peaceably alongside someone I really dislike for a cause that is decidedly unglamorous–it can be a tremendous challenge. Yet, this is what is required! The greater good is not reserved for a noble cause somewhere off in the distance. It is right *here,* right *now.* And while I fall short far more often than I'd like, I know that the only way I'll get better at it is by moving forward, by picking up the pieces and trying again.

The good news is that life is constantly presenting us with chances to do what is right. And most of the time, those chances are found right in our own backyards. Our ability to recognize and then act on these opportunities is one of the truest measures of character. So the next time your lab partner turns out to be someone you find irritating beyond measure, ask yourself if, just this once, you can dig deep and do what is required without complaining. Or better yet, at the next Christmas dinner, baptism or family reunion, summon the strength to spend time talking to an older relative, even if you don't find the conversation riveting. Ask them how they're doing and then take time to really listen to the answer.

The need to put aside our differences "for the sake of a greater good," as President Bush says, is a lifelong endeavor. In fact, it is a principle many of the men in this book put into practice when they chose to participate because, while they share many things in common—most notably and perhaps obviously, the fact that they are all men of character and integrity—there are probably more ways in which they are different than they are the same. Politically, racially, socio-economically and professionally, they represent a broad spectrum of the American experience. And yet, here they are, side by side, on these pages. Why? Because they know that you are all capable of so much more than you are sometimes led to believe, and they are willing to put aside whatever might otherwise separate them to help you see your potential. As members of the next generation, you embody their collective hope for a future that is better and brighter than anything we've yet seen and that hope is a cause worth coming together for. In other words, their "greater good" is *you*.

Ambassador Andrew J. Young, Jr.

Ambassador Andrew J. Young, Jr.

Photo credit: Michael A. Schwarz

An ordained minister and graduate of Howard University, Ambassador Andrew Young was a fixture in the Civil Rights movement alongside his mentor and good friend, Dr. Martin Luther King, Jr. He was appointed by Dr. King to serve as the executive director of the Southern Christian Leadership Conference (SCLC) in 1964, and it was in this capacity that he would help draft the Civil Rights Act of 1964 and the Voting Rights Act of 1965. A gifted strategist and negotiator, Ambassador Young often worked behind the scenes, securing agreement and compromise in situations most thought impossible. However, this does not mean that he escaped the brutality of that era. He participated in and helped lead marches across the South, suffering the violent consequences that accompanied them, and he was with Dr. King when he was assassinated in Memphis, Tennessee, in 1968.

Ambassador Young continued to serve the SCLC after Dr. King's death until 1970. He then served as a representative to the United States Congress (three terms), as mayor of Atlanta (two terms), and as the U.S. Ambassador to the United Nations.

He served as co-chair of the Atlanta Committee for the 1996 Olympic Games, and was instrumental in securing Atlanta's spot as an Olympic venue. In 1998, Dr. King's alma mater, Morehouse College, renamed its Center for International Studies the Andrew Young Center for

International Studies. The following year, Georgia State University renamed its School of Policy Studies the Andrew Young School of Policy Studies (where he currently teaches a course as a public affairs professor). He served as president of the National Council of Churches in 2000-2001.

In addition to serving on the boards of several Fortune 500 companies, Ambassador Young is a member of the President's National Security Council Advisory Board, is chairman of the $100-million Southern Africa Enterprise Development Fund, and remains active in numerous charitable activities and organizations, including the Martin Luther King, Jr. Center for Nonviolent Social Change. He is also the author of two books, *A Way Out of No Way: The Spiritual Memoirs of Andrew Young*, and *An Easy Burden: The Civil Rights Movement and the Transformation of America*.

Ambassador Young is the recipient of countless awards including the Presidential Medal of Freedom, the French Legion d'Honneur, and the Bishop Walker Humanitarian Award. He also holds more than 60 honorary degrees from prestigious universities worldwide.

The co-founder of the Atlanta-based GoodWorks International, Ambassador Andrew Young continues to travel extensively across the globe in his on-going work for peace and justice.

Editor's Note

When I went to Atlanta to meet with Ambassador Young, I did so with the understanding that our interview would last 30 minutes. I arrived early for my appointment; however, some last-minute demands on his schedule pushed our meeting back several times. Finally, his executive assistant came into the room where I was waiting and told me to grab my things and follow her. I did as I was told and, to my eternal delight, found myself accompanying Ambassador Young for the better part of the day as he moved from engagement to engagement. I watched him preach extemporaneously to a crowd for 30 minutes; I witnessed the grace with which he greeted every person who wanted to shake his hand (and they were many); and I saw his terrific sense of humor on display during a private lunch with his beautiful wife and three colleagues.

When I returned home and began to transcribe our interview, I found that my questions and comments most often seemed like awkward interruptions in an otherwise eloquent soliloquy. I quickly concluded that his words stood best on their own. Thus, while I have kept some of my questions and comments for clarity, by and large, I have chosen to simply "let the man speak."

I am honored to introduce one of the last surviving members of Dr. Martin Luther King, Jr.'s inner circle, Ambassador Andrew J. Young, Jr.

A Conversation with
Ambassador Andrew J. Young, Jr.

KHJ: When we talk about Martin Luther King or you or Gandhi—or any icon in history for that matter—we tend to think of people who were somehow different from us or, certainly, "better" than us.

Ambassador Young: Let me respond to that statement with a question I posed to the congregation earlier this afternoon. I asked them, "Was Martin Luther King a genius?" Of course the answer to that was a unanimous yes. I followed that up with a second question: Are you a genius? Are *you* a genius? Now the room got quieter; people were unsure of how to respond. But you see, if we say Martin Luther King was a genius without acknowledging that the same genius exists in ourselves, then we risk feeling relieved of the responsibility to pursue our own capacity for greatness.

Now, having said that, this book is for young men—and some people get mad at me when I say this—but I think it's normal for young men to be rough and tough. It's normal for them to be vulgar and rowdy and callous. It's normal to see them trying to be too cool and too hip. Saint Augustine—a *saint*—struggled with his faith and his conversion until he was 35! He said as a young man, "Save me, dear God; but not right now!" In other words, I *want* to follow you, but I'm having too much fun! (laughs)

Youth is a time of excess, and that is true whether you are a saint or Martin Luther King or whoever. And, by the way, Martin was a pretty wild kid. He had his struggles just like everyone else. He grew up in the YMCA and he was a good basketball player. But he always thought that he wasn't very good-looking and that he was too short. He had all sorts of color complexes and complexes about his hair—as all young men do! In fact, he was still struggling with some of these things when I met him, and I was struggling with my own things. So we struggled together in these "ordinary" things even as we made our way doing "extraordinary" things. But people look at Martin and they forget this.

KHJ: So how did two "regular guys" achieve such incredible things? How did you find it within yourselves to face the kind of hatred and very real, physical danger placed in your path?

Ambassador Young: Well, I was very lucky in that, at a relatively young age, I had what could be called a revelatory or divine experience. I was sitting on the top of a mountain in North Carolina and, as I sat there taking in the majestic view before me, it suddenly became clear to me that everything out there, *everything* I could see, had a place, and that there was a perfect order to everything. The sunflowers, the corn, the fields with the cattle–everything in the world had a place in God's order. And I knew also that there was a place for me in that order. I didn't know what that place was, but at that moment, I knew God had a purpose and plan for my life simply because *there was a purpose and plan for everything* in life!

From that moment on, my life has been at peace. And when I left that mountain top, everything began to unfold–everything from the jobs I had, to meeting my wife, to meeting Dr. King. From the moment in North Carolina to this day, my life has unfolded in order. The right doors have always opened . . . *eventually*. (laughs)

Likewise, the thing that I think set Martin apart was that he understood early on his power was not in the flesh, but in the spirit. He understood that he was not a human being who had occasional spiritual experiences; instead he was a *spiritual* being in the midst of a human experience.

Now certainly, we grew up fast during the fight for Civil Rights–there was a great deal of responsibility placed on all our shoulders. But the thing that really allowed us to overcome the tear gas and the dogs and the physical abuse was our faith in God. We had faith in God and we had a cause that sustained us. When you have those two things–there really are no limits to what you can do and what you can endure.

KHJ: That, to me, sounds extraordinary!

Ambassador Young: No, we were, as my daughter once described us: "just some get-down brothers in the right place, at the right time, trying to do the right thing." Do you know what we were doing right before he died? We were having a pillow fight! I came into the hotel room* after being in court and he laughed and said, "Where have you been?!" And he took a pillow off the bed and threw it at me. "You've been gone all day long. I don't know what you've been up to!" I said, "I've been in court!" Well, he grabbed another pillow and threw it at me, and by the time he threw the third pillow at me, I started throwing them back. Then everybody picked up pillows and we started in . . . anyway, that is what we were doing. A few minutes later, Martin walked out the door of the hotel room and was assassinated.

We were all headed out to dinner and I was in the parking lot when I heard the gunshot. Honestly, at first I thought someone was just playing around–with firecrackers or something. I called for Martin and when he didn't answer, I assumed he was playing a trick on me. But then I saw his shoe sticking through the railing of the balcony, and I knew. I ran back up the stairs and I saw him . . . and I knew he was gone.

KHJ: That must have been a devastating blow for you personally.

Ambassador Young: His death was shocking, yes, but it was not unexpected. He had foreseen his assassination. He knew it was coming, and he took it seriously. But, you know, he also used to joke with us about it. He would pretend to give us our eulogies because he said that the guys shooting at him were bad shots; and since we were always standing next to him, we were likely to go before he did! (laughs)

KHJ: Weren't you afraid?

Ambassador Young: The truth is that no, we were not afraid. We were ignited with passion for the cause of Civil Rights, and we fought for those rights using the dual powers of love and forgiveness. When you are filled with that forgiving love, you no longer fear. The most that they can do is kill you, and what is death but a pathway to heaven?

---

*The Lorraine Motel in Memphis, Tennessee, served as the makeshift headquarters for Dr. King and key members of his Southern Christian Leadership Conference who had come to Memphis to help organize peaceful marches in support of the Memphis sanitation workers' strike. It is now the site of the National Civil Rights Museum.

KHJ: *But weren't you angry when he died? I feel angry about the way he died, and I (obviously) didn't even know him.*

Ambassador Young: I was mad, yes. But at him! I said, "How dare you leave me here with this mess! How dare you go on to the Promised Land without me." I wasn't angry with his killer because, as Martin often said, there can be no resurrection without a cross. *This is how it is. We learn through our suffering.* Whether you're talking about Christianity or free enterprise, we know that you learn through failure. If you are succeeding at everything you're doing, you're not doing enough; you're not risking enough. It is not until you push the envelope that you have a breakthrough and new things happen.

Martin went to jail in Birmingham, Alabama, on a Good Friday, and when he went into that Birmingham jail, he did it because he thought the movement had failed! Everyone was convinced the movement had failed. The black leadership was telling him, "You have to leave here and raise money to bond our people out of jail." But he refused. He said, "I can't leave them. The only thing I can do is go to jail with them." While he was in jail, eight white clergymen published an open letter attacking him [for engaging in civil disobedience and urging him to allow the matter of civil rights to be resolved in the state and federal court system]. And it was then that he wrote his "Letter from a Birmingham Jail."* He wrote it around the borders of newspapers and on toilet paper and whatever scraps he could find to write on. Everything began to change after that. That's the cross and the resurrection!

Let me put it in football terms. You don't make a touchdown on every play. You know that when you go off-tackle and there's a big guy in front of you, sometimes you'll get by him; but most of the time you're going to get knocked on your behind. So you get back up and you try to go around him. And maybe you get thrown for a loss, but you get back up and you try again. You have four tries and then you have to give the other guy a chance. But you know your turn is coming back around. So football is a very good metaphor for life.

---

*Dr. King's "Letter from a Birmingham Jail" is widely considered one of the greatest historical, social and spiritual statements ever written. Within four months of its publication, a group of 250,000 supporters congregated in Washington, D.C., to hear Dr. King's history-making "I Have a Dream" speech. It was the largest civil rights demonstration in history. One year later, the Civil Rights Act of 1964 was signed into law.

KHJ: You said earlier that one of the things that allowed you to face danger and opposition without fear was your faith in God and the strength that came from having a purpose in your life that went beyond yourself, beyond self-interest.

Ambassador Young: Dr. King used to say that if a man hasn't discovered something he will die for, he isn't fit to live. In other words, if your world-view is dominated by *self*-interest, it's going to be a small world, and a petty world, and it's *not* going to get you through. There will be nothing to hold you up when the bumps in the road come–and they're coming!

Just take a look at the stars who walk the "red carpet"–practically every one of them has a screwed up life. Why is that? It's because their sense of validation comes from *outside* of themselves. The things that are most important to them are "self" centered: how they look, how they dress, how much money they make, how well their movie did. A few months ago, every kid in this city had a number 7 Michael Vick jersey. He was the ultimate success. A multi-millionaire! Then came the bump in the road. Now he's in prison; the crowds are gone; the amenities are all gone. You look at all he had, yet none of it can provide him any consolation. The only hope is for him to find something *within*. Malcolm X did. He went to prison and found his soul–or at least started the process. Mike Tyson didn't. Prison broke Mike Tyson. He was not able to put aside the external and find meaning beyond his own desires. His despair, which continues to this day, is a natural consequence of the choices he has made.

I don't know how to say it any more plainly. You are *not* simply this flesh and blood! You are spiritual beings, and because of this, you will not achieve the happiness you desire by living selfishly. You cannot survive like that!

Now does this mean you cannot be successful? Of course not. We formed this business, GoodWorks International, because we felt called to help American businesses get into Africa, and we have been very successful. But before we began, I asked myself–Does this feed the hungry? Does this clothe the naked? Does this heal the sick?–and it does. Business does that. Jobs and work and wages and prosperity do all of those things. Nevertheless, I get criticized all the time for associating with Chevron and Walmart. But to my way of thinking, it is very simple: if we want lights, we need oil. If we want to drive cars, we need oil. It is ultimately very hypocritical to want to live as we do and not want to associate with the companies that allow us to do it.

So I say by all means, be successful. Be as successful as you possibly can! But find a way to serve God in your work at the same time, either directly or indirectly.

In the end, what we do here [on earth] doesn't much matter. Our time here, whether it's 39 years as it was for Martin, or 90 years as it was for Benjamin Mays,* or however long our time is, it is short when measured against eternity. The bottom line is that we're *all* going to die. Maybe–*maybe*–you have something to say about when . . . but not much. But you have something to say about what you die for! And you have something to say about what you live for!

KHJ: *Do we have time for word association?*

Ambassador Young: Surely, yes.

KHJ: Compassion.

Ambassador Young: Love.

KHJ: Boys don't cry.

Ambassador Young: Crap.

KHJ: Bullies.

Ambassador Young: Weak.

KHJ: Respect for women.

Ambassador Young: Real men.

---

*Martin Luther King's friend and spiritual mentor, Benjamin Mays, served as president of Morehouse College (Dr. King's alma mater) from 1940 - 1967. Keeping the promise he made to Dr. King before he died, Dr. Mays delivered the eulogy at Martin Luther King's funeral.

Admiral Leighton W. Smith, Jr., USN (Ret.)

Admiral Leighton W. Smith, Jr., USN (Ret.)

Adm. Leighton W. Smith, Jr., is a retired four-star U.S. Navy Admiral and the former commander in chief U.S. Naval Forces Europe, commander in chief Allied Forces Southern Europe, and commander of the 34-nation NATO Implementation Forces in Bosnia (IFOR). Over the course of his distinguished naval career, he held command at every level in the naval aviation community, from squadron CO to commanding officer of USS *America* (CVA 66) to commander, Carrier Battle Group SIX. A light-attack pilot, he flew 280 combat missions in Vietnam, logged over 4,200 flying hours, and made over 1,000 carrier landings.

He is the recipient of more than 40 military decorations and international awards including two Defense Distinguished Service Medals, the Navy Distinguished Service Medal, three Legion of Merits, two Distinguished Flying Crosses, two Meritorious Service Medals, 29 Air Medals, the Order of Merit of the Republic of Hungary, and the French Order of National Merit (with the rank of Grand Officer).

Admiral Smith retired from active duty in October 1996. On March 5, 1997, he was made an Honorary Knight of the British Empire in a private audience with Her Majesty the Queen. He has since served in numerous civilian positions, including senior fellow for the Center for Naval Analysis, chairman of the board of trustees of the U.S. Naval

Academy Alumni Association, chairman and member of the Board of Trustees of the Naval Aviation Museum Foundation, and member of the executive committee of the Association of Naval Aviation.

In 2004, he was appointed by President George W. Bush to serve a three-year term as vice-chairman of the Naval Academy Board of Visitors. In 2007, the United States Naval Academy honored him with its most prestigious honor, the "Distinguished Graduate Award."

He is the president and founder of Leighton Smith Associates, an international consulting firm specializing in defense-related business. He also works closely with the Johns Hopkins Applied Physics Laboratory on the development of war-fighting technologies and serves on numerous corporate boards.

Editor's Note

Many folks hear the words "four-star Admiral" and immediately picture a stern, no-nonsense fellow, long on rules and short on humor. If you happen to be one of those people, then you're in for a surprise.

Admiral Smith is a gifted military commander known for his extraordinary ability to deal with "rapidly changing complex political and military"* environments under the most difficult conditions. But he is also gregarious, quick with a joke and unbelievably humble. In fact, when you're with him, it's easy to forget that you are in the presence of the same man who spearheaded NATO's relief efforts in Bosnia, served as the commander in chief of Naval Forces Europe and the commander in chief of Allied Forces Southern Europe, simultaneously. Frankly, he seems a whole lot more like the guy everyone wants at their table for dinner–which, in his case, is absolutely true.

Ironically, for someone who went on to become a highly decorated four-star Admiral, he came awfully close to never wearing the uniform at all.

So it is my great pleasure to present to you his essay on personal responsibility; or, as he would call it: "How I almost flunked out of the Naval Academy and became a pig farmer."

---

*Taken from the U.S. Naval Alumni Association & Foundation on-line press release announcing Admiral Smith's "Distinguished Graduate Award," http://www.community.usna.com/NetCommunity/Document.

Whose Life Is It Anyway?

I was never a good student.

In fact, I was a horrible student! In high school especially, I spent more time trying to figure out how to get around having to study than I did preparing for classes; and more often than not, I was successful. I talked my way out of tough situations with my teachers and basically spent three and a half years at Murphy High School in Mobile, Alabama, just "getting by." In the words of Murphy's assistant principal, Mr. Phillips, I was the only student he knew who had "talked his way through high school." But no one had ever pushed me–either at home or at school–to do better. When I graduated in 1957, I didn't have a clue what my grade point average was, and frankly, I could not have cared less.

Not surprisingly, my experience in high school led to a similar approach at the University of Alabama. In my first semester, I had a near-perfect attendance record at parties and football games and the miserable grades to prove it. On top of that, because I had no idea what I wanted to do "when I grew up," I had signed up for courses that really wouldn't have prepared me for a career in anything. And so, just as in high school, I barely scraped by.

In November of my freshman year, while home on Thanksgiving break, my dad commented that he had run into our local congressman Frank Boykin's administrative assistant and learned that the congressman was going to decide in February on his lineup for appointments to the various service academies (*e.g.*, the Naval Academy, Air Force Academy and West Point). As I recall, at that time each congressman could nominate one young man to each of the service academies as his or her "principal appointee." The congressmen usually selected two or three alternates in case his principal appointee did not pass the academic or physical tests. My dad said that if I was interested in going to one of the academies, I'd better get my name and some letters of recommendation to the congressman.

I had not seriously thought about going to any of the service academies up until then. My dad had tried to get me interested in the Naval Academy several years earlier because his brother Page had graduated from there and had gone on to have a very successful naval career. In fact, at that time my Uncle Page was a vice admiral and in charge of the Bureau of Naval Personnel. I suppose that this is part of the reason I ultimately warmed to the idea of the Naval Academy–this, and the fact that it presented an opportunity to do something totally different and to make a fresh start. It also was attractive because money was tight at home, and I knew that unless I worked, I had little chance of ever finishing college. So, when I returned home for Christmas break, I decided to gather up as many letters of recommendation as I could to try to get my name on Congressman Boykin's list of candidates.

Because our family had lived in Mobile for years and had many good connections, I had a long list of folks on whom I could call and seek support. When I left to go back to the University of Alabama in early January 1958, more than 60 people had promised to write to the congressman on my behalf. Interestingly, two of my teachers told me that while they would gladly write a letter, they knew I would never survive a year at the Naval Academy because I did not have the required academic underpinnings or the study habits that would be essential for that tough academic environment. I would later recall these dire warnings with good reason; but at the time I was just happy to get a letter from them.

In February, my Uncle Page called to inform me that he had just heard from Congressman Boykin's office; I had received the Congressman's principal appointment to the Naval Academy. I was ecstatic! However, when I shared my great news with my fraternity pals, I was stunned at their reactions. Almost to the man they asked me what the heck I thought I was doing. "You'll never make it through that place!" they said. Even one of my college instructors told me straight out, "Smith, you'll fall flat on your butt." Such encouragement!

At home, my father told me over and over how proud he was of me and that he knew I would give it my best shot. "But," he assured me, "if you don't make it, I will know you tried your best, and I'll be very proud of you for that." Frankly, I think he knew my chances of getting through the Academy were slim–after all, no one was better acquainted with my poor academic background and study habits than he–and he was trying to establish a cushion on which I could fall without busting my rear end too badly. Unfortunately, while I'm certain it was not his intention, he was also setting me up with an excuse to fail.

That summer, with all the normal doubts and fears that accompany a young kid about to embark on an entirely new experience, I took my first airplane ride, from Mobile to Washington, D.C. I was met by my Uncle Page and his wife, Dee. After a brief two-day visit, my Aunt Dee drove me up to Annapolis, Maryland, where I arrived at the Academy with nothing but the clothes I was wearing, a shaving kit, a check for $100 (required to be paid on entry) and a few bucks in my pocket. I will never forget standing in front of Bancroft Hall, the home for the Brigade of Midshipmen, for the very first time and thinking to myself, "What in the hell am I doing here?!" I began to hear the voices of those who had said I would never make it, and recalled what my dad had said about being welcomed home with open arms if I didn't. In short, I was beginning to doubt myself before I had even begun. It was the first step toward failure.

The days immediately following my arrival at the Academy were hectic: checking in, swearing to "uphold the Constitution of the United States against all enemies," meeting classmates (not knowing that 44 years later some of them would still be my closest and dearest friends), drawing gear, stenciling every stitch of clothing we were issued with our name and class, undergoing medical checkups, getting shots and haircuts, and receiving room assignments and schedules for the coming days. It seemed chaotic but, in retrospect, it had the benefit of leaving me very little time to worry about how (or whether) I could pull this year off. All of that changed very quickly, however!

My first exposure to the academic rigors at the Academy began with the start of summer classes. These classes were mandatory and were designed to prepare us for the beginning of the "real" academic year. Two hours into my first algebra class I realized I was in serious trouble. My professor did, too, and assigned me to what was then referred to as the "bucket class." The "bucket class," as you might have guessed, was for those students who were at the bottom of the barrel academically. I tried to convince myself that I was "giving it my all" in there, but the truth of the matter is that I wasn't. Consequently, I was little more prepared for the beginning of the academic year when September rolled around than I had been when I stood looking at Bancroft Hall on day one.

What started out badly went steadily downhill when our real classes began in the fall. The professors at the Academy were thoroughly uninterested in what academic preparation I had or did not have. They set their standards to reflect the requirements of the Academy and expected the midshipmen to work, however hard was necessary, in order to meet them. My lack of study habits became starkly evident and by early November I was in serious academic trouble. Of the five subjects we were required to take that first year, I was failing three and had a "D" in the other two.

As I recall I wrote home rather frequently, each time complaining about the very tough academic environment and making all sorts of excuses as to why I was doing so poorly. In none of my missives did I ever assume responsibility for the mess I was making of this once-in-a-lifetime opportunity. True to form, my dad would write back telling me how proud he was of me and how he knew I was giving it my best. "No matter what," he assured me, "you will be welcomed home with open arms by a very proud father." Again, without meaning to, he continued to make it easier and easier for me to fail.

I limped along certain that I was on my way out of the Academy—and *thinking that that was okay*. After all, it seemed that everyone except me had been pretty sure I would not make it. I was just up here "giving it my best," and proving them to be absolutely correct. That all changed when, out of the blue, I was summoned to the Office of the Commandant of Midshipmen.

This was not an event that any fourth-class midshipman looked forward to—especially one who was making a mess out of every course he was taking. But, I donned my best uniform, made sure everything was tucked and folded to perfection, and marched smartly to the reception area just outside the commandant's office.

I felt a level of fear that I had never before imagined. After all, the commandant is judge, jury and executioner at the Academy, and I knew there was a better than even chance that I would leave his office an *ex*-midshipman, on my way to pack up and return home. That is when it finally struck me that "going home" was *not what I wanted*.
I had been raised on a farm just outside of Mobile—the same farm

where my dad and his siblings had been raised. It was a good life, but a hard one in many ways. When we first moved in, our tiny house had no indoor plumbing, no hot water, and no insulation in the walls, floors or attic. The bedroom I shared with my two sisters was about the size of a modest walk-in closet. One of my jobs on the farm was tending to the livestock, which included cows, chickens and a few dozen pigs. I never did learn to milk the cows and I was attacked by the darn rooster every time I went into the chicken pen. But the worst animals, by far, were the pigs. They were ornery, they regularly escaped their pen, and they smelled so bad it made me sick just to be near them. As I waited to be escorted into the commandant's office, I suddenly pictured myself back in Mobile with no college degree and no job prospects–nothing except for that farm *and those damned pigs*.

I was jarred back to reality when one of the officers in the reception area pointed towards the door and told me to knock once and enter. I did exactly as ordered.

Seated behind a huge, polished, wooden desk, flanked on one side by our nation's flag and on the other by the Navy flag, sat the commandant of midshipmen, a very erect and incredibly imposing Capt. William F. "Bush" Bringle, Naval Academy Class of 1937. Captain Bringle was in his service dress blue uniform, not a wrinkle anywhere to be seen. On his chest was an impressive array of ribbons stacked row upon row nearly to the top of his left shoulder, leaving just enough room for the Navy pilot's Wings of Gold he had earned in 1940. The Navy Cross, second only to the Medal of Honor in recognizing heroic achievement and valor in combat, was particularly conspicuous atop all of his other awards. I knew that Captain Bringle had won his Navy Cross for heroic action in an aerial flight during the Allied invasion of southern France in 1944. He had also seen considerable action on the other side of the world in the Pacific at Leyte Gulf, Iwo Jima and Okinawa. Though I didn't know for certain, I supposed that at least one or two of the five Distinguished Flying Crosses he had been awarded must have been the results of his deeds during those intense battles in the Pacific. This man was a warrior!

A rugged face, stern expression and closely cropped graying hair were matched by the steely blue eyes boring into me. In a voice that conveyed both authority and concern, Captain Bringle ordered me to "stand easy." It would have been more plausible for me to fly to the back side of the moon than "stand easy," but I managed to assume the position of "parade rest"–a somewhat more relaxed position than that of attention. He reviewed my academic record (three Fs and two Ds), and I readied myself for the worst. To my amazement, it did not come. Instead, he posed a question–he asked me to tell him what sort of problems I was having. I started to give the standard plebe response of "I'll find out, sir!" but he stopped me short. Then, with almost fatherly concern, he asked, "Are you having a particularly difficult time with the upper classmen?"

I said that I was not having any more difficulties with the upper classmen than my classmates.

He then asked if my instructors were providing all the help I needed.

I responded that they were all good and willingly provided help when asked.

There was a pause while he studied whatever was on the paper he was holding. It was decision time.

I have no idea how long I stood there as he weighed his options, but I do know that in those few moments, many thoughts crossed my mind. It suddenly dawned on me that I had not only given up on myself, but I also had accepted failure as being, well, acceptable. I had listened to, and eventually had begun to believe, all the people who had said I would never make it. And now I was about to be told that they had been right. But the commandant was not of the same mind.

Captain Bringle finally looked up and said something I will never forget: "Midshipman Smith," he said, "you can do this!" These were not idle words of encouragement; they were an assessment. The commandant had looked at this farm boy and saw no reason why I couldn't do better. He believed I had the brain power to succeed at the Academy and he was not about to let me throw that opportunity away. He gave me 10 days in which to obtain satisfactory grades in all subjects and told me that if I failed to do so, he would see me back in his office. I responded with a sharp "aye, aye, sir," after which I was dismissed. I snapped to attention, made a smart right face and marched from his office.

As soon as the door closed behind me I made a promise to myself. *I would never, not ever, go back into that office under conditions similar to those I had just encountered.* However, in order to keep that promise, I had to do some serious soul searching. What I came to realize was that, not only was I the one responsible for the situation I was facing, I was the only one who could alter the outcome.

I began by seeking out help from classmates and instructors and, not surprisingly, found that they were all eager to help. In a short period of time, the help I was receiving, along with a serious dose of self-application, made a tremendous difference in my academic performance. I never became a star student, and I sweated out a number of finals while at the Academy, but my life became a lot easier once I finally realized *who was in charge of my life*. It was the guy staring back at me in the mirror!

Years after this event, a dear friend and wonderful, nationally recognized educator asked what had motivated me to go on from that session in Captain Bringle's office to not only graduate, but to have a successful career in the Navy. I laughingly replied that it was "those damned pigs," but of course it was more than that. In fact, it was the sudden realization that if I didn't take responsibility for my own life and commit to the work that would be required to succeed at this –the first true test I had faced as a young adult–that I would become accustomed to failure and accept it as part of my life. I also knew that I would spend the rest of my life making excuses or blaming someone else for my not "making it." I determined then and there that I would not allow those who had told me I would fail to be the ones who guided my fate.

I have long believed that my very brief session with Captain Bringle was one of most critical defining moments in my life. I will remain forever grateful to him for providing not only choices and options, but the real motivation that, quite literally, changed my course from failure to success. The Academy was, and remains, a tremendously competitive institution with hundreds of young men (and now, women) trying to cope in a totally new, different and frequently confusing environment. Yet in the midst of all of this and despite his myriad responsibilities, a real war hero and leader of men had reached deep down into the brigade to extend his hand to a midshipman who had all but given up on himself. For my part, it was the first time in my life that someone had told me, "You *can* do this! You are better than you think," and, more importantly, "It's up to you." To this day, it remains one of the finest examples of real leadership I've ever witnessed, and it altered the path of my life by opening my eyes to the fact that I was in charge of my own destiny.

The same thing is true for each and every one of you today—*you are responsible for your life and what you make of it. Period*! Not your parents. Not your teachers. Not your friends. I say this knowing full well that life is easier for some of you than it is for others. There are those who lead relatively charmed lives and others for whom every day may feel like a battle. Even so, the same rule applies. Is that fair? Hell no, it's not fair! But if you need life to be fair in order to move forward, then you'd better get comfortable right where you are. You will never effect meaningful change simply by wishing things were different, or worse, making excuses as I did. If you don't like the direction your life is headed, then decide to take charge and start making some changes. Oftentimes, the first step is to ask for help, as I had to do so many years ago. But however you begin, the day you can finally leave all excuses behind and take full responsibility for what you make of your life, you will experience a sense of freedom and purpose like you've never felt before. In other words, you'll be well on your way to becoming the man you were meant to be.

Tim Seibles

Tim Seibles

Photo credit: Chuck Thomas

A walk-on football player for Southern Methodist University, Tim Seibles had big dreams as a child, none of which included becoming a poet. But that all changed during his sophomore year when he took a creative writing class and discovered "a freedom in words that [he'd] never known in anything else." Tim received his B.A. in English from Southern Methodist University and, after a decade spent teaching high school English, went on to receive his M.F.A. from Vermont College.

Today, Tim is the award-winning author of six collections of poetry, including *Buffalo Head Solos, Hammerlock, Body Moves, Hurdy-Gurdy,* and the chapbooks *Kerosene* and *Ten Miles an Hour.* His work has also been featured in numerous anthologies such as *New American Poets of the '90s, Outsiders, In Search of Color Everywhere, Verse and Universe,* and *A Way Out of No Way.*

Tim has been awarded writing fellowships from the National Endowment for the Arts and Provincetown Fine Arts Center. In addition, he received an Open Voice Award from the National Writers' Voice Project and was a finalist in the Third Annual Library of Virginia Book Award for Poetry.

Tim is a frequent guest at poetry festivals and readings nationwide. When he is not traveling, you will likely find him at Virginia's Old Dominion University, where he is an associate professor in the master of fine arts in creative writing program.

Editor's Note

Tim Seibles looks like a football player–tall, strong, and broad-shouldered. As a child, he dreamed of playing in the NFL, and he pursued that dream all the way to Southern Methodist University, where his talent earned him a spot on the team as a walk-on. Ultimately his dreams took him in another direction; still, the size and athleticism of the ballplayer remain. So you can imagine the startled looks he receives when people discover that he is a poet.

Of course, that really just goes to show how little most of us know about poetry. Tim's poems crackle and vibrate; his is not the poetry "of a highfalutin' violin nor the somber cello, but a melody you heard somewhere that followed you home."* *Moving on a sea of syncopated rhythms,* Tim reaches across generations with the unvarnished truth about what it means to be alive–as an American, as a black man, and as a human being.

So, how did he get here? How did this kid who grew up in the turf wars of Philadelphia's infamous "Dogtown" make his way to becoming not simply a survivor, but an acclaimed poet and university professor? And, having come so far, what does he know for sure?

I am honored to introduce the coolest poet I know, Professor Tim Seibles.

---

*The Poetry Center at Smith College, http://www.smith.edu/poetrycenter/poets/tseibles.html (quoting Sandra Cisneros).

Hard-Headed

I was a hard-headed kid. I had a lot of energy and a crazy streak that made me a pretty rough customer for teachers–especially in high school, when I first felt the stirrings of manhood and began to think of myself as something like an adult. I didn't like homework. I didn't like spending hours in little wooden desks. I damn sure didn't like anybody telling me "what to do and when to do it." Of course, I wasn't the only one getting restless and impatient with adult authority; my best friends had their own itches to scratch and when we were together in any particular class, I bet the teacher cringed.

By the time I was five, I loved football. By tenth grade, I was sure I was going to play wide receiver for the San Francisco 49ers and be the best of all time. I even slept with my ball so that my hands would dream that shape, so I'd be able to catch anything under any conditions–rain or shine, icy or muddy. I watched NFL highlights religiously. I could see myself on TV *shakin' and bakin'* anybody who tried to tackle me. John Facenda's commentaries on the best plays were like messages from God guiding me toward the gridiron.

My parents thought I had lost my mind, which I had–partly. I just wanted to catch that ball and dance to the end zone. Playing football was about the only thing I always wanted to do, and truthfully, no matter how crazy I wanted to be in class, I knew that if I was going to play I had to keep my grades together. Back then, pro scouts didn't pay attention to high school athletes, so I knew I had to get to college to get noticed.

At the time, my friends and I were just young dudes imagining our names in lights. We didn't know that we didn't know very much about life. That's the thing about being a teenager: you find yourself–in a household, a neighborhood, a school–surrounded by all kinds of people, and because you're still learning who you are and what to do and who to trust, it's easy to believe that somebody else knows more than you do. That's why most teenagers get so serious about style.

Back in my high school days, I used to hate wearing the shoes my mom picked out for me just because they weren't the kind my friends had. She loved buying these big, clunky brogans, but the cool shoes were these sleek Italian kicks with intricate designs on the toes. Of course, the other guys were doing exactly what I was doing: trying to meet some standard of *hip* set up by somebody else. I was too young to have a clear sense of the game so, too much of the time, I accepted what other people said before I even considered my own opinion. I'd only gotten a small taste of life, so I thought in small, nervous ways when, in fact, life was filled with things I might do—beyond whoever or whatever was supposed to be cool.

I grew up in Philadelphia—Philly—in the Germantown-Mount Airy neighborhood: the turf of Dogtown, a gang with a reputation for ruthlessness. I saw the "warlord" once. I can't remember his name, but he had that I-know-I'm-bad look in his eyes and big biceps that made it pretty clear that he could probably back that look up. Luckily, I lived there, so if one of the soldiers ever stopped me to ask, "Where you from?"—meaning what part of town or which gang—I could say, "Right around the corner," and be pretty sure there wouldn't be any beef. Most of my friends and I thought it was stupid, even then, to beat people or kill them because they lived in a different neighborhood. But corner gangs were serious business, and if you didn't want your ass kicked—or worse—you had to pay attention to where you were.

I did have a friend who was a member of the Haines Street gang. We weren't close friends, but we knew each other from 10th grade English class and clowned around some. The Haines Street mark was a blended H and S, which made a dollar sign, and Jeff drew it on his books, his school desks, on just about anything. You'd also see that dollar sign spray-painted on the sides of buses that drove through their turf.

One afternoon after school I was standing at the bus stop and one of the Haines Street oldheads walked up to me. An oldhead was usually out of school, a full-time gang member. (We didn't call them gangsters. In the movies, gangsters wore pinstripe suits, carried submachine guns and battled the FBI.) Anyway, this guy comes up to me wearing a small, golden dollar sign earring and asks, "Where you from?" He had a big scar running from his left cheek down to his chin, like he'd been slashed in the face not too long ago. I knew I was closer to Haines Street than I was to Dogtown, so I answered, "Nowhere," which was a way to back down without looking like a chump.

Now, usually this was enough—you let the tough guy show his power, and then he would let you slide peacefully. But this guy responded, "Seem like nowhere's gettin' to be a pretty big corner," as if "nowhere" was another gang. This meant I wasn't going to get the normal break. Of course, I'd been in fights before but never with a gang member and definitely not with an oldhead. Things were looking pretty bad: I thought, at best, I would probably get knocked down; at worst, I could get stabbed. I think the oldheads did this kind of thing to make sure nobody thought they'd gone soft. I know he must have seen the fear in my eyes, but I couldn't run; that just meant I'd get my butt kicked on another day. "Showing some heart" and fighting might've gotten me some respect or maybe just thoroughly stomped right then and there. I was thinking fast. Only a few seconds had passed, when out of nowhere, Jeff walked up and said, "Let him go, Stone, he's cool," and the dude left me alone. Stone's full name was Headstone because, according to Jeff, he had killed somebody. It was simple luck that I'd been in class with Jeff—and real luck that he'd been nearby when Stone was ready to pounce. He told me later that Headstone had ended up in a wheelchair because of a gunshot wound. Who knows what scars I would have today if it weren't for Jeff? Who knows if I'd even be here at all?

I mention this story, not just to show what my teenage years were like or to give Jeff credit for stepping up but because, over the years, I've thought about Stone and all the other young brothers like him—who ended up crippled or hooked on drugs or in prison or dead because they believed that being a hard guy was the cool way to roll. No doubt, their friends had a lot to do with why they took that road. I know that schools are not always ideal places for learning. I had classmates who struggled with grades for awhile, then just gave up. Sometimes certain schools make it hard to dream. I also know that if you are black or brown the challenges you will face are, in most cases, different from those faced by your white counterparts, particularly considering how prejudice can eat away at anyone who is the target of bigotry. But I also know that before someone turns into a "Stone" he has to lose sight of himself. He has to give up on the idea that his life might become something positive and important. I don't mean to suggest that this happens easily or suddenly. The collapse of hope and the erosion of belief in self take place slowly over a number of years in both visible and invisible ways. However, I also feel certain that having faith in yourself and having a sense of your own worth don't come easily or suddenly either. They are things that you have to fight for every day, in spite of the fact that the world is big and often unfair and, in many ways, makes it difficult to see the things inside you that could make your life remarkable.

I never got to play pro football. I played a little in high school and for a season in college before it became clear that I was not destined to dazzle the NFL. This did bring me down for awhile. I'd be lying to say I wasn't disappointed, but I don't think those dreams of gridiron glory were a waste of time–not at all! Wanting to be a professional athlete kept me doing my homework and away from gangs and drugs and other kinds of trouble. Of course, girls weighed heavily on my mind. We were all burning for romance and we were teenagers when miniskirts first came on the scene–but I knew I didn't want any surprise children. I didn't want my life tied up before I got to do what I really wanted to do, so I was very careful. I was all about protection for myself and for any girlfriend I had.

Having big-time dreams pushed me to learn discipline: if I was going to be a star I had to practice, lift weights, and continue to believe that *I* was someone who *could* be a star, someone whose life was going to matter–no matter what. The hard-headedness that sometimes made me trouble for my parents and teachers also made me hard to discourage. After my football dreams faded, I didn't know what or who I might become, but I kept thinking I was supposed to do *something* that stood out. Because I had kept my grades up for football, I found myself in college where other roads opened to my life, roads I could never have taken if I hadn't made it to college. I knew college meant study, study, study; but it also meant getting away from home and getting a fresh look at everything.

I had no idea that I would become a poet, but I took a creative writing class in my second year of college and discovered my mind: my own heart and imagination. There was a freedom in words that I'd never known in anything else. Nobody could tell me what to write, because no one could know what *I* needed to say. The realization that each person has a unique perspective, that *I* had a unique perspective, made me want to look more and more deeply into my mind and more carefully into what was going on around me. I began to believe I could see what other people missed, that I could fill in some of the blanks that troubled people. I could write about anything and no one could stop me. My body couldn't fly, but my words could. Language became a kind of vehicle that had unlimited speed and unlimited range. When I wrote, the feeling was something like the feeling I had with a football in my hands, except that my destination, my goal was different in every poem. I could address the most terrible or beautiful things. I could deal with racism, love, loneliness, war, cartoons, the planets, sports—and, if I wrote well, others could see what I saw, hear what I heard. I was amazed that poetry had been here all along, but I had never gotten a real sense of its sharp edges, its wild potential. After one semester in a writing workshop, I was nearly obsessed with poems.

This doesn't mean that I was a good writer. I must confess I was a pretty lame poet in those first years. My writing professors must've read my stuff, shook their heads, and wondered what I thought I was doing. They were polite when criticizing my work, but they could not have had any idea that I would actually become a published author. My enthusiasm must've been pretty obvious, but I didn't really know anything about writing. I had no real understanding of what poems could do, but I found myself full of passion for poetry and, with that fire in my heart, there came the will to work harder and harder. Word by word, I began to understand that writing was a way *to find out exactly what was in my head*, and it turned out that there was a lot going on in there—a lot more than I ever would've guessed.

I was 19 years old when I began to take writing seriously. Now, I've published six books and I teach writing at Old Dominion University. If someone had told me back in high school that I was going to be a poet and an English professor, I would've thought they were crazy. I could only see my future as a series of game-breaking touchdowns. I see now that it's way too easy to underestimate what's possible in your life. As a young man, I thought of my future in terms of one dream, one possible way to make it. But the future is always made up of choices, doors to be opened—doors that lead to other doors that lead on still to others. The only thing any of us can do is try to pursue what we love and trust that, in the heat of that pursuit, we will discover a way to use our talents to satisfy ourselves and also to be of some positive use to the society we live in. If I hadn't worked hard in English class because I wanted to get to college for football, I wouldn't have had the language skills I needed for poetry. In an odd way, football showed me the door to my life as a poet and teacher. The fire that lit the grass under my feet became the fire that lights the page when I sweat over the words and sentences that help me make sense of the things that rise up inside me. Every step we take counts in ways that are often hard to see. Everything you do connects to all that you might do. Every poem grows out of the first word.

Here's an early poem that I wrote for a friend of mine. We grew up playing football in the neighborhood playground. It was only two-hand touch, but we played like our lives were on the line.

NOTHING BUT FOOTBALL
for Melvin Strand

Brother, those days in the schoolyard
playing football with the sun
preaching heat to the asphalt, when
we thought everywhere was Sharpnack Street
those were good days: you and me
and all the moves we used, our feet
fast and smart as angels, our heads saved
from everything but dreams
of getting the ball and that single
glorious, ever-present possibility of *touchdown*.

Our sneaks, laced with *NFL Highlights*,
with a football in our hands we were
right as priests: celibate, heaven clearly in sight,
ready to abandon the world, just to get closer
just to fake the hell out of anyone
trying to stop us. They couldn't stop us—
you stutter-stepped, I snake-slipped, anything
to spin-shimmy away clean as light, slick
as sweat: what hymn, what hidden rhythm
did we dance to then?

I hated to play against you, trying to read
the mystical sermons of your feet, the blur
of your *Converse* high-tops, that sudden cut
that always came sure as dark, and the finishing
gallop that left us praying to your back.

A Better Man

There was nothing more beautiful, no
creature more untouchable its escape,

and I have loved nothing and no one more
than those summer days
when we roamed the schoolyard
beyond our parents, riding a football
into this life—every day
a new game, every catch a blessing,
every opening   a parting of the sea.

--Tim Seibles

Ray Allen

Ray Allen

Photo credit: Nike, Inc.

NBA veteran Ray Allen knows a thing or two about making history. Widely regarded as one of the best "pure shooters" ever to play in the NBA, this nine-time NBA All-Star is second on the NBA's all-time list of three-pointers made and the twenty-third player in NBA history to drain 1,000 three-pointers. In 2006, Ray broke the record for most three-pointers made in a season; he shares the record for the most three-pointers made in one half. He also holds the record for most seasons leading the league in three-pointers made. His skills were never more evident than in the sixth and final game of the 2008 NBA Championship when he tied the NBA Finals record for three-pointers made in one game (seven), broke the record for three-pointers made in an NBA Finals series (22), and helped his team bring home the championship trophy.

Ray played for the University of Connecticut and graduated as a first-team All-American and the recipient of the Big East Player of the Year award. Taken fifth overall in the 1996 draft by the Minnesota Timberwolves, Ray was traded to the Milwaukee Bucks, where he made an immediate and enduring impact. In 2003, he was traded to Seattle, where he would begin to see his name be etched in the history books. But it was his 2007 trade to the Boston Celtics that would provide Ray the opportunity to reach the pinnacle of his sport.

Ray is consistently ranked in the top 10 among free-throw shooters in the league with an average that hovers near 90 percent. He scored a career-high 54 points in one game in 2007 and has a career average of over 20 points per game. He was named honorary captain for UConn's All-Century Team in 2000. In 2008, he was honored again when Milwaukee fans voted him number three on the Milwaukee Buck's list of the "20 greatest players in franchise history." He was also a member of the 2000 Olympic gold medal-winning U.S. men's basketball team.

Ray's honors and accolades extend well beyond his skill on the basketball court. He received the NBA's prestigious Joe Dumars Sportsmanship Award for the 2002-2003 season, and he has twice been named one of *Sporting News'* "Good Guys" (2000, 2001). He is a member of the All-Star Advisory Council for the Jr. NBA and Jr. WNBA basketball support programs, an NBA spokesman for the Thurgood Marshall Scholarship Fund, and the founder of the Ray of Hope Foundation. He is also a member of Nike's Air Jordan brand.

A true Renaissance man, Ray also has starred in two films, including Spike Lee's *He Got Game*, for which he received strong critical reviews.

Editor's Note

From all outward appearances, Ray Allen and I have very little in common. So you can imagine my surprise when I realized that our opinions on several key issues were virtually identical. Whether we were discussing the role of women in society, the question of contentment, or the movie Schindler's List, *I found myself strangely in sync with this man I barely knew.*

I also discovered something about Mr. Ray Allen: he has a genuine gift for extemporaneous speaking. No matter the topic, his words flow easily, logically, and at times, almost poetically. It was clear that he had given a great deal of thought to the issues we discussed (and had done so long before we had ever met), and he managed to infuse his answers with both eloquence and passion—a combination that is none too easy to pull off.

It is my distinct pleasure to introduce the wise and very eloquent, Mr. Ray Allen.

A Conversation with Ray Allen

KHJ: *Before I do anything else, I want to congratulate you on your championship win with the Celtics!*

Ray: Oh, thank you. I appreciate that.

KHJ: *For every kid who is out there spending those hours on the court, working toward that dream, could you describe what that feels like?*

Ray: Well, a lot of people have asked me and truthfully, it's one of those things where there's not a feeling you can compare it to. It's such a unique experience that you can't tell *what* you're feeling. And everybody feels something different. It means something a little bit different to each person. But when you win a championship like that, I think you can't help but reflect back on all the tough times you went through. You think about all the people who said you couldn't do certain things or achieve certain things, and all of these emotions start welling up in your body because here you are on a grand stage—and it's a verification of everything you set out to do in your life.

KHJ: *It must have been incredible to be there on that floor when the buzzer sounded, knowing that you had won the NBA Championship. If you think back to when you were a kid just learning to dribble and then bring yourself all the way up to that night—it's an incredible culmination. And it must have made everything you had done—all the thousands of hours of practice, all the times when you were the last one in the gym—it must have made it all seem worth it.*

Ray: I just got out of the gym, in fact, and I was the last one there. So it never does stop. The one thing that you really learn out of the whole process is that the feeling is not as great and huge as you might have imagined it, because once that night is over, once you walk away from that night, you've got to do it all over again. You're now *expected* to achieve greatness.

So, you learn very quickly that being a champion is not about winning the championship. That won't sustain you. It won't make you content. Being a champion is about how you live your life. It's about how you take care of your business every day; it's about how you deal with people, how you are in your community. It's about your habits in those things; and practicing those habits every day is what makes you a champion. And if you're fortunate enough to be around people, or in my case to play with 12 people, who have those same habits, then that is a real championship. You've hit the jackpot.

KHJ: *That's an interesting way to look at it because I think most of us look at something like winning the NBA Championship the same way we look at winning the lottery. We think, "Man, he's got it made!" And we assume that contentment and happiness just come with the territory. But your experience tells you that those things come from a totally different place.*

Ray: Absolutely. In my case, that night–that win–was for the year. From winter to spring to summer to fall–it was a compilation of many different places and people and it came to fruition on one night. But you win over the course of a year. And you only win, literally and figuratively, if you have the right habits in place, day after day, on the court and off it.

KHJ: *And, of course, people see you both on and off the court. Young men especially, I think, watch you and they look up to you for any number of reasons. Some may see a great ball player and a great competitor; others see just the money or the philanthropy. But the real question for me–and for you as well, I imagine–is this: What do you hope they see when they look at you?*

Ray: I want young men to see that life is not about the flash and flair. It's about having an impact on everything around you from your family to your community to the earth. At the end of your days, that inevitable question will rise within you of how well your life was spent. How well did you leave this planet from the time that you were born to the time that you left?

Ultimately, in my profession, we're playing a sport, and that is what the focus is on. But we're playing a sport that has seen great players before, has seen great players in our time, and will see great players when we're gone. So we can't reasonably be judged by our athleticism or by the numbers we put up or the championships we win. What we will be judged by–and judge ourselves by–is how we dealt with our success. How did you come across? How did you make the people around you better? Ultimately, that is what I want kids to see–that this game, like everything else in life, is about the relationships you create. Because once you're gone, that is what is left. That is what you take with you to sustain you and that is how you ultimately will be judged. *What did you do to make things better?* That is the question your life has to answer.

KHJ: *If some of the kids who look up to you could look inside your life –your daily life–what would they see you doing that reflects that?*

Ray: Number one, they would see the relationships I have in my life are with people from all ethnicities and all backgrounds. They are not necessarily celebrities or well-known in the community; they are people from all walks of life–people who I feel make me a better person. Two, I think from the standpoint of my job, they would see me approaching it *as a job*. I come at it in a professional manner. I'm good at it because I take care of it and I prepare for it the same way every single day. I don't use or abuse my job. I don't say, "This job is entertainment and I want to be on TV or I want more money or I want more women or I want to drive fancy cars." All that, from A to Z, comes with the territory if you love what you're doing. If you're passionate about what you're doing, you're probably gonna make a lot of money, and then you're going to become attractive to more women and get to drive the car of your choice, et cetera. But that is not the end game. No matter where you are, no matter what time is on your hands, you've got to get up and prepare for your job the same way. There's not one moment where you can take a break.

KHJ: *I know you only mentioned women in passing, but I'm going to take advantage of that if I can. I think women get a bad deal in terms of how they are portrayed in the media. And, I think it shortchanges not only them, but men as well.*

Ray: I agree.

KHJ: So then, what is the difference between the way our culture depicts women and the way you view women?

Ray: First and foremost, I think there is a limited value placed on the importance of a woman's role in society. That goes back hundreds of years. Women are just as important to this world as men. I believe a woman has the same abilities as a man.

My wife and I were just talking about this last night—we have two boys and we have a third baby on the way—due in July sometime—and she was telling me that she thinks [this third one] is a boy. And I said I think it's interesting because I think God puts children in our world based on what the man has gone through. So if a man has been a womanizer his whole life and done certain things that are disrespectful to women—you see so many of these men having daughters. Case in point: I see a lot of men in professional sports having daughter after daughter—and when I see that I say to myself, "Man, he must have been hard on women during his life!" (laughs) I have two boys and if I get a third boy, as I told [my wife], I think God knows I'm ready for the challenge of raising men to really protect women and to take care of women and to show women that they are coveted and cherished. And [to show them] that they are valuable for things that are real—not for what we see in our society.

KHJ: Is that way of thinking about women something you had to learn or is it something you've always known?

Ray: I was raised by my mother and three sisters, so I grew up respecting women. I show women respect regardless of whether I come across them in business or in my personal life because I want people to respect my mom and I always want people to respect my sisters and my wife. I expect men to treat them properly because that is what I demand of myself and it is what I have always done.

KHJ: As a woman, I think the lack of respect really becomes a problem when we see young women being portrayed as commodities more than as individuals. When you look at the way women are used in media, you can see why so many young men have this idea that it's cool to sleep with a woman and move on. But this getting together for a night or two and disappearing and then getting together with another woman and disappearing—it does such damage. And I'm not talking about morality so much as harm on a human level, because when you treat other humans as disposable or as commodities, you do harm to them. And to yourself for that matter. At least this is my belief.

Ray: I agree. And it becomes a vicious cycle because what inevitably happens is that you end up having kids, and they grow up seeing that kind of behavior. If it's a daughter, she grows up to be a woman who dates men who don't treat her the right way because she doesn't know how men should treat her. And if it's a son, he's going to grow up to be like his dad. That story repeats itself generation after generation.

The same is true for criminal behavior and for abuse—most of the people in jail were mistreated as children. So, when it comes to women, I think every man in this world should take the time to make a woman feel better. The good men need to make up for the ones who aren't doing the right thing. When you see a woman walking across the street—she could be a teacher on her way to work with 30 kids for six hours, and if you compliment her or help her across the street, she's going to go to school with that little bit of extra energy for those kids. Or it could be someone's wife—someone raising children—and that is what society says is our foundation. We hear a lot of concern, "The children! The children!" But children start with a man and a woman, and with a man taking care of a woman. That relationship is so critical, and we don't teach that. We don't take it seriously like we should. Ultimately it will be our downfall.

KHJ: *I read in several places that your favorite movie is* Schindler's List, *but I could not find any interviews or bios that say why. It is a tough movie and so, of course, I wonder what about it inspires you to name it as your favorite?*

Ray: It is a tough movie. I watched it the first time as part of an independent study project in college. When I walked out, I had tears [in my eyes]. I thought, "Wow this guy [the main character] as much as he was selfish in the beginning, he really got it and he realized that [the Holocaust] was about human kind, and about human decency. And he began looking around at things and seeing that, for example, the ring he had [could have bought safe passage] for five people or that his car could have helped 20 people. It was about the simple act of deciding to care about the next human being.

We don't do that. We look at the world and see people of different ethnicities, different backgrounds, different living conditions. We could all take a page from Schindler's play book. He started out seeing himself as a German, but in the end, he saw himself just as human. So he was reaching out to help the Jews, but really he was reaching out one human to another.

KHJ: *Why do you think it struck you so deeply?*

Ray: I was raised in the military and we lived in Germany, England and all over the Americas. So I had the good fortune of experiencing different cultures, different scenes. I think maybe I already had a sense from my childhood that even though people have different points of view and different ways of looking at things, no matter where you go you're going to find generally the same mix of folks–good, bad and indifferent. The [Holocaust] happened decades ago, but all of its lessons are relevant. Globally they're relevant when you look at Rwanda and Darfur and other places, and individually, they are relevant to how we can each choose to act in our lives.

I've gone to the Holocaust museum four times. I've taken a different person with me each time because I think the lessons are that important. I took one friend of mine recently and his reaction was, "What about slavery?" I told him, "This has nothing to do with slavery and everything to do with slavery. This is the Holocaust. It is a lesson in how you treat your neighbors and how you treat people who are different from you. It is a lesson in what happens when we lose our sense of decency and our humanity." That was what I wanted him to see.

KHJ: *If you could go back and talk to your 15-year-old self, what would you say to him?*

Ray: It's interesting that you ask that because I was watching a show on TV the other day where they were talking to a prisoner–an older man–and he was sitting in his cell, and he was talking about how he wished he could go back to when he was 25, to when he had shot and killed someone he thought had stolen from him. That one decision cost him his freedom for the rest of his life. When I speak to young men I tell them that when you get older, you're going to say, "I wish that at 20, I'd have taken care of the man at 50." And that was what this old man in jail was saying. He was saying, "I wish that the 25-year-old me had taken better care of the old man."

I feel like the 15-year-old me did a pretty good job of taking care of the man I am today. So I would tell him to keep doing what he's doing, keep doing what's right.

And now my job is to take care of the 50-year-old man.

KHJ: *Are you ready for a short word association?*

Ray: Sure. Let's hear it.

KHJ: *Bullies.*

Ray: Short-lived; insecure.

KHJ: *Compassion.*

Ray: We all need it.

KHJ: *Respect for women.*

Ray: If you want a full life, if you want people around you who care about you, then you'd better respect women.

KHJ: *Boys don't cry.*

Ray: If you've ever loved another person or have been loved, then you have cried.

Colonel John W. Ripley, USMC

Colonel John W. Ripley, USMC

Col. John W. "Rip" Ripley, United States Marine Corps, was a man of uncommon courage and is widely regarded as one of America's greatest war heroes.

A 1962 graduate of the United States Naval Academy, he was the recipient of six valorous and fourteen personal decorations, including the Navy Cross, the Silver Star, two Legion of Merit awards, two Bronze Star Medals with combat "V," and the Cross of Gallantry with Gold Star. He was, in fact, one of the most experienced Marine commanders of his era. During one of his tours in Vietnam, Colonel Ripley was wounded on four separate occasions. He "refused evacuation on the first three managing to avoid the paperwork and 3 Purple Hearts which would have mandated his removal from the fight. Seriously wounded a fourth time, Ripley was forced to evacuate but upon recovery insisted he be returned to his Company to complete the mission of leadership to his men."* His unparalleled heroism during his many years in combat left him riddled with so much shrapnel that pieces of it continued to surface from his body throughout his life.

---

*Taken from the citation accompanying Colonel Ripley's induction into the U.S. Army Ranger Hall of Fame.

He was most famous for single-handedly blowing up the bridge at Dong Ha, Vietnam, a feat so perilous and so far beyond the normal limits of human endurance, that it has been described as "the most extraordinary act of individual heroism of this war or any war."* His valor in destroying the Dong Ha Bridge during the 1972 North Vietnamese Easter invasion is memorialized both in the book *The Bridge at Dong Ha* and in a large diorama on permanent display at the United States Naval Academy's Memorial Hall.

In 2002, Colonel Ripley became the first Marine officer to receive the Distinguished Graduate Award, the Naval Academy's highest and most prestigious honor. Four years later, in July 2006, the Naval Academy Prep School at Newport, Rhode Island, christened its newest building Ripley Hall in his honor. In June of 2008, he made history when he became the first Marine inducted into the U.S. Army Ranger Hall of Fame, an honor reserved for "the most extraordinary U.S. Rangers in American history."** Later that same year, he traveled to Devon, England, where he was inducted into the Royal Marine Commando's *Royal Marine Association*–the first American ever to receive this honor. Back in the states, his hometown of Radford, Virginia, declared Veterans Day 2008 "Colonel John Ripley Day."

The most telling honor of all, however, may be one that did not make headlines. In May of 2004, when the 22nd Marine Expeditionary Unit established a forward operating base in one of the most hostile and remote sections of Afghanistan, the marines assigned to the base chose a name that they felt would reflect the courage that would be required to survive there. They called it "Firebase Ripley."

---

*From "Ripley at the Bridge," a diorama on permanent display at the United States Naval Academy. For a riveting account of Colonel Ripley's heroism at the bridge, read *The Bridge at Dong Ha* by John Grider Miller (Annapolis: U.S. Naval Institute Press, 1996.)

**U.S. Army Ranger Association, The Ranger Hall of Fame, http://www.ranger.org/html/ranger_hall_of_fame.html

Editor's Note

I received the news that Colonel Ripley had passed away at his home in Annapolis, Maryland, shortly before this book went to press. Needless to say, his death came as a shock, and it has left a gaping hole in the lives of all of us who were lucky enough to call him a friend. While it is true that he was a legendary marine possessed of unimaginable courage, he was also a man of uncommon kindness and extraordinary humility–a man who was, as his daughter described him, "a better father than he was a marine."

And a better friend as well. I will miss him greatly.

I wrote the following introduction several months before he died and have chosen to include it here in its original form:

As you might expect, Colonel Ripley is, in many ways, an imposing presence in person. Yet, if you were to go looking for him, I'd be willing to bet you would have a hard time picking him out of a crowd. I say this because, despite what we have been led to believe on TV or in the movies, real heroes don't go around kicking ass and making noise. They don't lurk in dark corners waiting to spring into action or spend their free time looking for a fight. When they are called upon to act, they do so without hesitation–and sometimes violently –but they come and go quietly. No Hollywood blaze of glory; they just do their job and move on.

I've had the opportunity to get to know Colonel Ripley a little bit over the years. He exhibits the best of contradictions, exuding both a steely self-confidence and an unabashed selflessness. And while he is tough as nails when it comes to discussing topics like courage and integrity, should the conversation turn to his hero, Jesse Owens, or to his ailing wife, Moline, his words begin to catch and his eyes glisten.

True to his character, when I first contacted Colonel Ripley about writing for this book, he agreed to my request without hesitation. Despite being in the midst of a difficult and painful time in his own life, he shouldered the burden. And so, it is my great honor to present to you this essay on courage, from one of the most extraordinary men I've ever had the pleasure to know.

Uncommon Courage

There are certain basic elements that exist in every person—man, woman, or child. As certain as you were born with muscle, blood, and bone, you also were given a standard issue of courage. While this may seem unlikely to you because your opportunity to exercise this courage is somewhat limited, it is there nonetheless. Courage is a concept without a physical form that resides in you. While you cannot see it, you can see the effects of courageous behavior. Indeed, we often are in awe of someone who performs a courageous act, and almost always admire and respect them for their actions.

There are several different kinds of courage. The one we are most familiar with is physical courage. We call it "physical courage" because it is based on a physical act—a person must make a conscious decision to actually *do* something that puts them at risk—often great risk. Who can forget the scenes shown on television when the firemen and policemen of New York City moved into the World Trade Center after the terrorists had slammed aircraft into the Twin Towers? Many of these brave first responders gave their lives in a final, conscious decision to try and rescue the people trapped inside.

Physical courage is as close to "tangible" as courage comes. It can be readily seen and easily understood. But there is an altogether different kind of courage—what I would call moral courage—that is rarely seen, even less well understood, but equally deserving of our respect and admiration.

Like physical courage, moral courage requires you to make a conscious decision. Though you may not be putting life or limb on the line to act in a morally courageous manner, there are other risks involved that may be very precious. Indeed, like physical courage, moral courage often involves real sacrifice. You must be prepared to give up something that is important to you, and you never really know beforehand the extent of what you may lose.

Imagine, for example, that you are with a group of friends and one, or several, suggest doing something that is wrong and likely to get you in trouble (whether it is painting graffiti on private property or another more serious act—throwing stones at passing cars, assaulting someone with a weapon, and so on). If you are a person with a high degree of self-confidence and self-control, you don't have a problem when you find yourself in one of these situations. You simply say, "That's not for me. I don't do that, and I don't hang out with people who do." Then you go on your way.

But things are not always this simple. Most of us, when we are young, simply don't have this kind of confidence. Instead, we fear that if we speak up, we will lose our reputation as "one of the guys," or worse, that our friends might turn on us: they might accuse us of being a Mama's boy or threaten us physically. In these instances, demonstrating moral courage can be a daunting challenge because it demands sacrifice. However, based on a lifetime's worth of experience, I guarantee you that regardless of the way your friends and peers react at the time, they will respect you for the values that you have the courage to exhibit and for taking a stand on an issue you know and *they know* is right. Surely you have seen examples of this in school when someone takes a stand, especially an unpopular stand, and then holds their ground in the face of insults and attacks? A person of courage will always be respected, and *respect*, as everyone knows, has a far greater value than *friendship*.

And what about bullies? Every school has a few. These are the kids who try to gain the attention and respect of others through threats and intimidation. They enjoy trying to push around those they consider weak (kids who, by the way, are almost always smarter than they are). But every so often something great happens; to everyone's surprise, another student, boy or girl, has had enough and jumps in to stop it. It is usually someone who not one soul would have suspected had it in them to do such a thing! Yet they come forward aggressively and put an end to the harassment. In the end, they gain the respect of almost everyone, even if it is a silent respect, *which it almost always is*.

I have little doubt that each of you, if asked, would say that when you grow up you would like to be well respected—a man of courage and compassion, someone who treats his fellow human beings with dignity. But in life, the right thing to do is rarely the easy thing to do and, in the end, your ideals are *meaningless* if the decision to act in accordance with these ideals comes only when there is little or nothing at risk. Courage, whether moral or physical, always comes at a risk and with the *expectation of sacrifice*. It never comes cheaply. The world is full of timid souls who seem willing to go through life never taking a stand or coming to the aid of those in need. They avoid risk at all costs. By contrast, a person who takes action and who jumps in to stop the harassment of another knows he risks being attacked himself. But his courageous action demonstrates to everyone watching that the behavior he stepped in to stop was completely repugnant and against the values of every decent person.

I want to close by telling you about one of my all-time heroes, a man of great courage named James Cleveland "Jesse" Owens. Jesse Owens was an athlete—a runner—who came from nowhere and had nothing. As a young man, he was put in a position where his nation's and his own reputation were placed at risk before the entire world and it was up to him to defend both. The son of an Alabama sharecropper and grandson of a slave—Jesse Owens' moral and physical courage were so profound that, in my estimation, he is one of the greatest men the world has ever known.

Jesse grew up terribly poor in a home that was not much more than a dirt floor shack. He was a sickly child who rarely had enough food to eat or proper clothing to protect him from the elements. At one point when he was young, he developed a life-threatening abscess that would surely have required the amputation of his leg without an operation. Jesse's family was too poor to afford a hospital; so, while his father held his struggling son, Jesse's mother performed the operation with a kitchen knife that she had heated in the fire. Young Jesse displayed enormous courage while his leg healed—and what legs they would become! His running ability in high school ultimately earned him a place on the Ohio State University track team—a huge accomplishment for a black student at that time. But Jesse's greatest moments were yet to come.

Jesse Owens would reach the pinnacle of his athletic success during the 1936 Olympic Games, which were held in Berlin, Germany. These were times of great international concern, as Adolf Hitler had achieved total power in Germany and had created his Nazi state, a state that he was directing headlong into World War II. He wanted the Berlin Olympics to be a showcase for his Aryan "Master Race" —a term that included white ethnic Germans but almost no one else —certainly not racial minorities like Jesse. Hitler's Nazis scorned America for having black athletes on its Olympic team, calling them "black auxiliaries" or worse, "non-humans." However, Jesse and his black teammates showed their character and moral courage by ignoring these comments. They answered Hitler's ignorance and hate with remarkable performances on the field. In particular, in just 45 minutes, this remarkable American, Jesse Owens, demonstrated to the world all that could ever be known about moral courage, grace under pressure and the heart of an American. He would enter four events and win the gold medal in each, becoming the first American track and field athlete ever to win four gold medals in a single Olympic games.* In this stunning performance, Jesse Owens tied the Olympic record in the 100-meter dash, set Olympic records in the long jump and 200-meter dash and broke the world record as a member of the 4 x 100 relay team. Jesse's performance was so remarkable that the 110,000 German people in the Olympic Stadium rose to cheer him, clearly upsetting the prancing, posturing Hitler who subsequently left the stadium to avoid the humiliation of the awards ceremony where Jesse and his teammates would be honored.

In every event that day, Jesse Owens could feel the incredible pressure to represent his country—and himself—honorably. He knew that any failure on his part would serve to reinforce Hitler's racist views, while letting down his team and his country. The pressure had to be enormous. But in less than one hour, this one-time sharecropper's son, this young boy without enough food or clothing, this man who had defied the odds, this stunningly remarkable American and athlete earned the admiration of the world when he not only delivered a record performance but did so with the utmost grace and honor.

I believe that Jesse Owens is the greatest American athlete of all time —far greater than those we see today—because he overcame such adversity to perform in circumstances no athlete today can even imagine. He had courage of the soul and of the heart. Today we would recognize him not just for his extraordinary athletic ability, but for the richness of his character, and his determination to win with honor.

---

*Jesse's record stood for almost 50 years. It was broken in 1984 by Carl Lewis.

He was a man who could perform at his best in the midst of great adversity, while the world—almost literally—stopped and watched. We must never let his memory fade.

Today in Berlin there is a street named for Jesse Owens. The man Hitler and his Nazis despised is now a role model for German youth! He should be that for you as well. This is the courageous American every one of us should aspire to be. And while we may never reach the athletic achievements of Jesse Owens, each of us can, in our own lives, demonstrate the same moral courage that he showed to the entire world back in 1936 when he stood alone on the world stage and embodied courage, grace, and the true measure of a man.

Kenny Leon

Kenny Leon

Kenny Leon is a highly acclaimed director, producer and actor whose experience covers the spectrum of television, stage and film. He has directed numerous Broadway plays including the recent revival of *A Raisin in the Sun*, starring Sean Combs, Phylicia Rashad, Sanaa Lathan and Audra McDonald. The production garnered two 2004 Tony Awards and went on to register the highest-grossing weekly box office sales for a drama in Broadway history. A film version of *A Raisin in the Sun,* which Kenny also directed, aired on ABC in February 2008.

Kenny also has directed all 10 plays in August Wilson's Pittsburgh Cycle, including the 2004 Broadway production of *Gem of the Ocean* (five Tony nominations) and the 2007 Broadway production of *Radio Golf* (four Tony nominations). In addition, he has directed extensively at theatres across the country, including, among others, Chicago's Goodman Theatre, Boston's Huntington Theatre, Connecticut's Long Wharf Theatre and Hartford Stage, Baltimore's Center Stage, Los Angeles' Center Theatre Group, the Milwaukee Repertory, New York's Public Theatre, Atlanta's Fox Theatre, the Seattle Repertory, Georgia Shakespeare, the San Jose Repertory, Dallas Theatre Center and Oregon Shakespeare.

In May 2004, he was chosen as one of *People Magazine's* "50 Most

Beautiful People."

When Kenny is not on-location shooting a movie or directing on Broadway, he can be found in Atlanta at True Colors Theatre Company, which he co-founded and where he serves as artistic director. He also serves on the Obama Arts Policy Committee, the American National Theatre Advisory Board and is a member of 100 Black Men of Atlanta.

Editor's Note

I first met Kenny Leon in a crowded, outdoor Atlanta café where our interview was nearly drowned out by car horns, passing trucks and one very loud couple seated to our right. We both wondered whether the recorder would manage to pick up our conversation amid all the auditory debris. Thankfully, somehow it did. We talked for a little over an hour before Kenny had to leave, first for a live television interview across town, then to catch a plane to Los Angeles for a meeting with actor Laurence Fishburne. Or was it Morgan Freeman? Maybe it was Sean "P. Diddy" Combs. I can't remember. This vagueness of memory has less to do with my powers of recollection than with Kenny's nonchalance about the upcoming appointment. But, then again, Kenny is one of those rare individuals who is enmeshed in Hollywood star power without being remotely impressed by it. He is a gifted theatre director and has produced a staggering number of critically-acclaimed, award-winning plays through the years. Kenny directs plays not simply because he enjoys it; he directs plays because he loves it. And because he is passionate about it! He believes that theatre has the power to profoundly impact our lives.

Following his universally lauded film version of A Raisin in the Sun *in 2008, Kenny easily could have pursued a career as a full-time filmmaker, with all the money and glamour that the job implies. Based on his track record of success, it is hard to imagine he would not have become the next Ron Howard or Spike Lee. But he did not. Instead, while he still directs films here and there, he returns again and again to the thing that he loves most. All of which is to say that he has chosen happiness over fame and fortune. How many of us can say we would do that?*

I am honored to introduce a man who is both more talented and more fun than any one person has a right to be: my friend, Mr. Kenny Leon.

To Forgive

The following essay is taken both from a speech Kenny gave at the Tampa Performing Arts Center as well as from our conversation at that crazy-loud outdoor café.

I am extremely grateful for the life that I have. I love what I do for a living: running a successful theatre company and directing films and Broadway plays. I have had the privilege of working with some of the most talented and glamorous folks in the entertainment industry. And I am proud to number people such as Samuel L. Jackson, Angela Bassett and Sean "P. Diddy" Combs, among my friends. But life was not always this way. In fact, my childhood was about as far from glamorous as you get.

When I was young, I lived with my grandmother in Tallahassee, Florida, deep in the country. My mother, who was very young at the time, had left me in my grandmother's care while she went to try and build a life for me and my younger brother and sister. At my grandmother's house, we chopped wood for the stove, killed chickens for supper, had an outhouse for a bathroom, and reused the same bath water in a foot tub. The minister came only on the fourth Sunday of each month. There were not a lot of amusements that deep in the country. There were no Nintendos, Play Stations, Game Boys, Palm Pilots or BlackBerries. But I was *happy*. In fact, my grandmother filled my life with so much joy that I never even realized we were poor! We would sit together on her front porch for hours, talking and laughing. I've never laughed as much with anyone in my life as I did with her. Every single day I'm trying to live a life that is worthy of my grandmother's memory a life clear on values, clear on spirituality, clear on respect, clear on purpose and clear on passion. Everything that exists at my core today is there because of her.

My grandmother grew up when segregation was a fact of life for black people. Though she lived to see the success of the Civil Rights Movement, she was no stranger to the racism that lingered long after the 14th Amendment to the Constitution became law. A change in the law was a good step–an important step forward. But obviously it didn't change the way some folks thought about black people. In spite of this–maybe *because* of it–forgiveness and compassion were more than platitudes to my grandmother. They were a call to action and a challenge from God! She had an extraordinary ability to forgive and to extend compassion to others. Day by day, she taught me that we are all brothers and sisters and that things like age and race should not separate us.

I was in ninth grade when the civil rights laws took effect. I had moved back to live with my mother by that time, and here I was, this poor black kid from the sticks and I was being bussed to one of the wealthiest, white high schools in the county. It was a tough time–a *tough* time. Yet by my senior year I was voted president of the student body. People are always amazed by that and, over time, I've come to appreciate what an unusual end to the story it is. But it was not altogether unexpected from my point of view because I simply carried my mother's and my grandmother's lessons with me into that school environment. Seeing my mother's strength and determination to raise her children while working a full-time job gave me the strength I needed to make it through school. I decided that if she wasn't giving up on me, then I certainly wouldn't give up on myself! I also kept my grandmother's lessons in my heart: I looked for ways to build bridges. I refused to indulge hatred, and when I encountered it, I told myself, "That person may think he hates me because I'm black or poor or whatever, but he really doesn't. He just doesn't know any better." And I chose to forgive . . . I *chose* it.

Listen, we all make some terrible mistakes. There's not one grown person on this planet who hasn't done things they deeply regret. So forgiveness is a necessity for each and every one of us. In one of his last plays, Athol Fugard wrote that the two most difficult things for human beings to do are to ask for forgiveness and to grant it to others. Those are the two biggest, hardest things to do! And yet we *must* learn to ask for and to grant forgiveness because the inability to do so leaves us utterly vulnerable to the negative effects of pride, anger and hate. And the chasms between us grow larger. We become a society of "us versus them" until we can't even remember who we really are–a human family, children of the same God. Black, white, old, young, straight, gay, rich, poor, city dwellers, country folks: we all have a place at the table. We all bleed the same blood and breathe the same air. And so we *have to* continue to look for the things that bond us and find ways to move forward together as a culture and as a world.

I had the opportunity to travel to South Africa a few years ago and, while I was there, I became inspired by people like Desmond Tutu and especially by Nelson Mandela. Here was a man who had spent 27 years in a one-room prison cell. Why? Because Mandela was black and he had dared to demand equality. When he gained his freedom and he and his group came to power, they had to make a choice. They could spend the rest of their lives exacting revenge on their former captors or they could offer them forgiveness. Nelson Mandela chose forgiveness. After 27 years of degrading and humiliating treatment, he offered them his forgiveness! So, it seems to me that making the choice to forgive a hurtful remark or whatever kind of mistreatment that might be directed at me in my life is the least that I can do.

As co-founder of a large theatre company in Atlanta, I am trying to carry out the legacy handed to me by my mother and grandmother and by people like Nelson Mandela, by producing plays that expand the human spirit. I am passionate about my work because I believe in the power of theatre to change lives. And if I were to hand you a brochure about True Colors Theatre Company where I work, you would not find it filled with language speaking to the need for artistry or entertainment in the community. Instead, the company's stated purpose is "to celebrate life by exploring and understanding our differences and our commonalities." The four core values of the company are boldness, laughter, abundance and respect. And we make an open promise to the larger community that we will use our gifts "to seek truth and clarity. We will tolerate, encourage, explore and honor difference. And we will listen to each other."

We make these promises because they are the essential tools we must use if we are to uncover the truth of our common humanity. This is how we move forward. This is how we bridge the divides. We are a country at war with one another and with the world, and we are so easily divided along lines of class, politics, region, culture, race, and religion. The ways to divide will never end unless we *choose* to end them. But each person must choose it for himself. Look for what we have in common and honor what makes us different! Reflect on the past, examine the present, and contemplate the future as individuals, as a community, as a nation and as a part of the world. I promise you there is a place that crosses racial, cultural and religious barriers where we can truly feel a sense of community, but we have to be willing to work for it, fight for it, pray for it.

You owe a responsibility to everyone who lived before you to discover what you're supposed to be on this planet. You have a responsibility to find that thing that feeds your soul and makes you excited about being alive because when you do, you will find that you are acting from a place of integrity, from your heart. Then you become a bridge builder, a healer. This is true whether you are a doctor, a teacher, an artist, an engineer . . . or a poor, black grandmother raising her grandson out on a farm in Tallahassee.

I leave you with this, an excerpt from the monologue of the character Mr. Styles, from the play *Sizwe Bansi Is Dead* by Athol Fugard. Mr. Styles, a photographer, has recently photographed several generations of one family for a family portrait, or "Family Card," as it is called in the play. This scene takes place in Mr. Styles' studio the day the cards are picked up:

> *The moment he walked through that door I could see he was in trouble. He said to me: "Mr. Styles, we almost didn't make it. My father died two days after the cards. He will never see it." "Come on," I said. "You're a man. One day or other every one of us must go home. Here . . ." I grabbed the cards. "Here. Look at your father and thank God for the time he was given on this earth." We went through them together. He looked at them in silence. After the third one, the tear went slowly down his cheek. . . .*
>
> *You must understand one thing. We own nothing except ourselves. This world and its laws, allows us nothing, except ourselves. There is nothing we can leave behind when we die, except the memory of ourselves.*

Be passionate. Be forgiving. Live lives worthy of remembering.

Father Hector LaChapelle

Father Hector LaChapelle

Photo credit: LaChapelle family

Father Hector LaChapelle is a Roman Catholic priest and member of the Order of the Missionaries of La Salette. He was ordained in 1968 and has since worked in several states throughout the country, including North Carolina, Florida, New York and Minnesota. He spent several years working as a counselor at the Hazelden Foundation, one of the country's premier substance abuse treatment centers. He also helped develop and facilitate theological, moral, scriptural, social justice and pastoral programs in the Eastern and Midwestern areas of the United States. In addition to his regular duties, he also served as chaplain to the Minnesota Vikings from 1984 to 1990.

Father Hector currently serves as rector of St. Brendan of the Navigator Catholic Church in Shallotte, North Carolina. He also serves as theological advisor with the Pave the Way Foundation, an organization dedicated to ending religious hatred and intolerance.

Though Father Hector calls North Carolina home, he is an avid world traveler, and has toured extensively throughout France, Italy, Israel and Egypt.

Editor's Note

I realize that including a chapter on faith may be risky. Faith is, and always has been, a hot-button issue; it seems that no matter what you say, you inevitably offend someone. The following interview is no exception. However, in my opinion, faith is ultimately about having a belief in something larger than ourselves. It is that which calls us to look beyond the small corners of our lives and to see the world against the backdrop of eternity. This, I think, is worth exploring.

Finding the right person to talk with, however, was challenging. I imagined it would be someone outside the mainstream—a monk or a Buddhist priest, perhaps. To be perfectly honest, I didn't imagine for a second that it would be a Catholic priest. But when my parents mentioned in passing that the priest at their Catholic Church had recently invited in a Jewish speaker to educate the congregation about the inherent integrity of all world religions, I knew this was someone I wanted to meet.

They say that something extraordinary happens when you are in the presence of a truly holy person—that you cannot be close to them without being affected in some way. Go online and you'll find countless accounts, from people of every religious persuasion, of what it was like to be in the presence of someone like Mother Theresa or the Dalai Lama.

I have never been in the room with either of those world figures, so I am not here to make comparisons or bold claims. All I know is that there is a sense of lightness about Father Hector that stands in stark contrast to the heavy burdens of the world. When I am with him, I am transformed. My fears subside, the world makes more sense and I am acutely aware of that which is holy.

I am honored to introduce to you the most surprising Catholic priest you're ever likely to meet, Father Hector LaChapelle.

A Conversation with Father Hector

KHJ: *A lot of young people struggle with faith–young men especially. Would you agree?*

Father Hector: Oh, it's more than a struggle for many of them I'd say! (laughs) A lot of young people reject faith outright. It doesn't make sense to them, or they put their faith in technology or science because they feel it explains things. But faith does matter. You know, your soul is part of your birthright as a human being; it *belongs to you*, not to anyone or anything else. So you may reject a religion or the imperfections and missteps of a religion. But *faith*? Faith is yours alone. And that is a distinction people often fail to make. They assume faith and religion are one and the same.

KHJ: *I also think that, frankly, a lot of young men don't see faith as particularly "cool" or "manly."*

Father Hector: That's true. But you know, by and large, the greatest and most admired people throughout history were people of faith. They had a sense of their place in the universe. So, whether it *seems* "manly" now or not, that is the direction one ultimately wants to head in. All the worldly appetites that we have can be fulfilled, whether it is for food or sex or whatever. But we all also have an appetite for the infinite and of that, we can never have enough. We are all searching for that which can satisfy us at the deepest level and that is God or the infinite–call it what you want. Understanding this is, I think, critical to your survival. It is wisdom we all must come to accept if we are to live our best, our fullest life.

KHJ: *Okay then, let's talk about God. And if you'll permit me, I'd like to begin our discussion with the sticky subject of religion! In the U.S., we have Christians, Jews, Buddhists, Hindus, Muslims–I could go on. In short, you name it, we've got it. This isn't too surprising given that our country was founded in large part on the idea that there should be freedom of religion; and yet, we continue to divide along religious lines. Especially when I hear language like "chosen people," "the one true faith,"* or "the one path to God,"—whether it is coming from a Muslim, Christian, Hindu, or Jew—I get the feeling we each think we have an "in" with the Creator. I have to say, Roman Catholicism is right there in the thick of it.

Father Hector: Well, let's begin with the premise that God is much bigger than what we've made Him. I think we have to start with that because it is so critical to our understanding of everything else. We try to put God in a box; we try to trap Him. But He is beyond anything we can contain. This is our starting point.

Going back to your question, I think you're right in saying that different religions often want to claim superiority in some way over one another. If you think back, go back several thousand years ago to when we had the wrong framework for the way the sun, the earth and the moon moved in relation to one another, you'll remember that it took a Copernican *revolution* to change people's way of thinking! I think that in much the same way, we are due for a *religious* revolution in terms of the way in which we view God and religion.

KHJ: *How so?*

Father Hector: Well, I am a Christian, so I'll use that as an example. Many Christians today see the world as being Christocentric—a universe where Christianity is in the center and the other world religions exist in relation to it. [These other religions] are out there, but they exist in some "lesser" way. The same framework is in place for Muslims who view Islam at the center or Jews with Judaism at the center and so on. This is one framework.

Then you have a different framework over here—a theocentric framework —where God is in the center and all the different faiths (Buddhism, Christianity, Hinduism, etc.) exist in relation to God. In this framework they are all recognized as equal pathways to God. They all lead up the mountain. This is how I view the world. This is my framework.

KHJ: *Mine also. But why is it yours?*

Father Hector: Because I believe we *all* have a little bit of the truth. None of us has it all! And because as soon as we *think* we have the total truth —we can't have dialogue. We just want to proselytize and convert others to what we believe. Or if we can't convert them, then we condemn them or we go to war or proclaim them cut off from God's salvation or whatever. When we get to this point, we have completely lost our way. We have made God in our image, instead of the other way around.

KHJ: Just out of personal curiosity, how do you square a theocentric framework with the oft-quoted language from the Gospel of John, "No one can come to the Father except through me."

Father Hector: Oh boy, I knew that was coming. (laughs) First, there are a lot of different ways to interpret that quote. Let's go way back to St. Irenaeus, one of the early church fathers. He had what he called the "recapitulation theory." Speaking from a Christian perspective, the recapitulation theory begins with the premise that God and man were separated through sin, but that through the incarnation–through the very fact that God entered into our history and became one with human kind in the person of Christ–the *whole* of human kind was reconciled back to God. Thus, in a sense, salvation is "through Christ" because Jesus redeemed the whole world, the whole of human kind. Everyone and everything is included.

From this point of view, the language "no one can come to the Father except through me" is not construed in any narrow sense that I have to become a Christian, I've got to be baptized, I've got to do X, Y or Z. Instead, the whole world is sacred! There are an infinite number of ways to "come to the Father." The Druids encountered God in the trees–it was a sacramental thing for them. God was present for them in that tree! All the world speaks, and God reveals himself through everything. There is nothing that is out of God's reach.

This is my interpretation.

KHJ: I like it! Thank you. How do you, as a Catholic priest, interact with people of different faiths? When you are together, how do you handle your differences? Do you respect them by remaining silent? Do you try to reconcile these differences?

Father Hector: First, I believe there is one God, whether you call Him Allah or God or Spirit or whatever you want to call Him. As Christians, our primary holy text is the Bible. But, I believe that the Koran, which is sitting here on my shelf, also is a holy text. Like the Hebrew Scriptures

–it is a record of how God has spoken and acted through Muslim history as interpreted through the eyes of faith. It is inspired; there's a morality in there, a path to God. It maybe is not the way I understand it; but is it valid? Yes! Is it real? Yes!

I don't think God has revealed himself only in our Bible. That's what I mean when I say we limit God too much. In the same vein, again speaking as a Christian, the primordial sacrament for me is Jesus. But the whole world is a sacrament, so human beings can encounter God through all kinds of things.

KHJ: *What is a "primordial sacrament?"*

Father Hector: A visible sign through which one encounters God. For me, this is Jesus. But if Jesus is the visible sign of God's presence in the world, and if His spirit lives on in us through the church and through the "people of God" (meaning *all people*), then when you experience love through me or forgiveness through me, Christ or God is revealing himself through me. You encounter Christ in, with and through me just as I encounter God in, with and through Christ because he lives on–an extension of him lives on through time and space. His mystical body remains present to us and reveals itself to us through the world.

It follows then that whenever you encounter truth, whenever you encounter love–whether it's through Christianity or through Islam or through Judaism–you are encountering God. You are encountering God Himself.

KHJ: *Would the pope agree with you on that point?*

Father Hector: Pope John XXIII* would have! (laughs) I'm not sure about this pope, [Pope Benedict XVI**]. I knew him long before he was elected pope. He is extremely bright and he was quite liberal as a young man. But the 1960s came around with students rioting and protesting, just like they were in the states, and I think it affected him deeply. And his reaction was to become extremely conservative. Anyway, that's where he is coming from today, unfortunately.

---

*Pope John XXIII served from 1958 until his death in 1963. He is remembered as a pope of great warmth and charm who worked to make the church more accessible to its people.

**Cardinal Joseph Ratzinger was elected Pope in April 2005 following the death of Pope John Paul II. Upon his election, he chose the name Pope Benedict XVI.

KHJ: As a country at war, it sometimes feels to me like that is where almost everyone is coming from! I can't imagine being a young person, especially a young man, coming of age during all of this. The idea of Christianity and Islam and Judaism [and the rest] all being valid paths to God seems to fly in the face of most everything we read in the papers and see on TV about all the different conflicts in the Middle East.

Father Hector: Yes, but the message *is* there! And it has always been there. You find it in some form in every holy text. Look at the Gospels and the New Testament—Jesus is *totally* inclusive, regardless of race, religion, sex, social status. He was showing us that God isn't interested in these things, but by how much compassion and mercy we can [extend to others.] End of story.

There's a play by Jean Anouilh that tells of the last judgment. In the play, at the end of time, God says, "Everybody come into heaven!" And the so-called "good people" start grumbling, "Wait a minute. He can't do that! All my life I went to mass, never took the Lord's name in vain, never ate meat on Fridays, didn't commit adultery and on and on. Now you're saying that everybody gets in!" And in the play it is revealed that, in fact, *that* moment is the final judgment. The final judgment was not when God opened the gates of heaven to everyone, but instead, it was the moment after. It was the moment they failed to love.

In the end, the only way we're going to be measured is by how much we love God and love our neighbor. And in that moment they failed to love their neighbor in not wanting them to share in God's salvation.

What a great play. A great message.

KHJ: That reminds me of one of my favorite quotes from the Dalai Lama: "My religion is kindness."

Father Hector: Wonderful!

KHJ: Tell me about someone you admire.

Father Hector: Hans Kung.

KHJ: Who is he?

Father Hector: He is a Catholic priest and a writer—he's written all these books here [points to a bookshelf full of books] plus many more. He wrote these enormous volumes on Islam, on Judaism. He is, I believe, the greatest Catholic theologian of our time. But he has a long and complicated history with the Catholic church; he advocates a theocentric framework, he has criticized the papacy. It's a long story.

Anyway, as a result, he can no longer teach as a Catholic theologian. Yet, he is *still* Catholic and he is *still* a priest! [Goes to find a particular book.] He wrote in this book about why he is still a Catholic—why he has stayed in the church that has *silenced him*. Here is what he said:

> "... I draw hope out of faith, that as in the past, the cause of Jesus himself is stronger than all the misconduct in the church. In spite of everything, for the sake of the cause of Christ, it is worthwhile to be involved in the church as well as in active ministry."*

He is a man of unbelievable moral courage—just incredible . . . an incredible human being! He wrote another book that I have here in which he demonstrates all that we have in common with Buddhism, Hinduism, Islam, and Judaism, of course. It's fabulous.

The "truth" is that we are all God's children. All equal in God's eyes. We tend to want to make God's love conditional: "If you do that or don't do that, you will be punished." But God is all-inclusive; He excludes *no one*. He is all loving. He loves us not because *we* are good, but because *He* is good. His goodness, His love transforms us. I like to say that God is not on our back—he's on our side. And it is all gift, all grace. *Everything* is a gift. We live in a world of entitlement, but it is all a *gift*. We're forgiven, so we are called to forgive. We are loved, so we are called to love. Everything we've been given we are called to share with others. Total. Everything.

KHJ: Will you join me in some word association?

Father Hector: I'd be delighted to. Go ahead.

KHJ: Compassion.

---

*Hans Kung, *Reforming the Church Today: Keeping Hope Alive* (Edinburgh: T. & T. Clark Publishers, 2000), 12.

Father Hector: "Having undergone suffering with," literally translated. So my answer would be Jesus—the model of compassion.

KHJ: Boys don't cry.

Father Hector: Nonsense. Human beings cry.

KHJ: Bullies.

Father Hector: Insecure.

KHJ: Respect for women.

Father Hector: Again Jesus—respect for the individual and for who they are.

Commander Paul E. Galanti, USN (Ret.)

Commander Paul E. Galanti, USN (Ret.)

Paul Galanti was on his 97th mission as a Navy light attack pilot during the Vietnam War when his A-4 Skyhawk was shot down over Vinh, North Vietnam, and he was taken prisoner. He was sent to North Vietnam's infamous Hanoi Hilton prison complex, a horrific place where seemingly innocuous acts like sharing food or communicating with a fellow prisoner were grounds for grueling torture sessions. It was, as he says quoting his good friend and fellow POW John McCain, "organized inhumanity on a greater scale than [he] had conceived possible." It was also the place Paul Galanti would call home for seven years.

Commander Galanti's military decorations include the Silver Star, two Legions of Merit with combat "V," the Meritorious Service Medal, the Bronze Star Medal with combat "V," nine air medals, the Navy Commendation Medal with combat "V," and two Purple Hearts. He has appeared on the covers of *Life*, *Time* and *Newsweek* and in several documentaries, including the *Discovery Channel's* Emmy-award winning *Vietnam POWs, Stories of Survival* and Public Television's *Return With Honor*. He is also the recipient of numerous awards including the Liberty Bell Award and the Outstanding Virginian Award. In 2005, he was inducted into the Virginia Aviation Hall of Fame. And in 2007, Paul and his wife, Phyllis, who spearheaded the MIA movement in the 1970s, were honored when plans were unveiled for construction of the Paul and Phyllis Galanti Education Center at the Virginia War Memorial.

Commander Galanti retired from active duty in 1983 and went on to achieve extraordinary success in a variety of executive positions. He served as Virginia chair of Sen. John McCain's presidential bid in 2000 and as the chair of Virginia Veterans for McCain in the 2008 election. In 2005, he helped found the Families of the Wounded Fund (FOTWF), with a small group of other Vietnam-era military veterans. The FOTWF is dedicated to providing financial support (including lodging, food and other services) to families of combat-wounded patients being treated at McGuire Veterans Hospital in Richmond, Virginia. True to form, 100 percent of the monies donated go directly into the fund, while the founders pay all administrative, banking and other expenses out-of-pocket.

Editor's Note

To truly appreciate Comdr. Paul Galanti and what he has to say, you have to somehow come to appreciate the magnitude of what he endured during the many years he lived as a prisoner of war in Vietnam. I had done enough research to know, for example, that he and his fellow POWs were routinely subjected to torture sessions that had been designed to inflict excruciating physical and mental damage. I also knew that the sessions lasted for hours or days at a time. I asked him about it once because I simply couldn't imagine how he had managed to not let the relentless suffering destroy him. I was prepared for any answer except the one I got: "It was a pain in the neck," he said matter-of-factly. "And it pissed me off. But we all knew the worst that could happen was that they'd kill you. Then you were lucky–you got to go home." The only thing he admitted to finding a challenge was isolation, which he described as "pretty rough." So you can only imagine how horrific that must have been.

He wasn't being glib with his answers–far from it. In fact, the courage and fortitude with which he spoke that day staggered me. I felt as if I got a glimpse of the Paul Galanti former Vietnam POW Capt. Dick Stratton describes in his essay, "The Boat School Boys." Captain Stratton was shot down in January 1967, almost seven months after Commander Galanti had been taken prisoner. He was beaten, tortured and placed in isolation in the same prison where Commander Galanti was being held. Each day, several prisoners in the isolation wing were assigned the duty of collecting and washing the dishes and buckets used to serve their once-daily "meal." This was the only human contact Captain Stratton had those first few days in his cell. In his essay he describes what happened next:

> These guys would do the dishes, buckets and their armpits taking their sweet old time, making a hell of a racket and yacking away at each other to beat the band. But wait a minute, they were not talking to each other, they were talking to the rest of us as if they were talking to each other. . . .

Commander Paul E. Galanti, USN (Ret.)

"If you read me, cough once for yes; twice for no."

Cough.

Are you Air Force?"

Cough. Cough.

"Are you Navy?"

Cough.

"Are you an 0-5?"

Cough. Cough.

"Are you an 0-4?"

Cough.

"Oh sh___, another Lieutenant Commander! "Do you know who won the Army Navy game?"

Cough. Cough.

"Oh hell, a dumb Lieutenant Commander at that! Jim Stockdale and Robbie Reisner are the [Senior Ranking Officers]. Their rules are: communicate at all costs; when they get around to torturing you, hold out as long as you can, bounce back and make them do it all over again; don't despair when they break you, they have broken all of us; pray."

Cough.

... "My name is Galanti–Paul Galanti."

BANG! The universal danger signal, as I found out later. [Paul Galanti] was hauled out of the cell block, tortured, and I did not see [him] for three years.

I am honored to introduce you to one of the bravest men I know: my friend, Comdr. Paul E. Galanti.

"No Such Thing as a Bad Day . . ."

I was a Naval Aviation attack pilot during the Vietnam War. That's tailhook aviation. (Tailhook aviation is really just a short-hand term for those of us who were nuts enough to take off and land on aircraft carriers moving at high speed across the water.) I flew 97 missions over North Vietnam and 96 went according to plan. But on my 97th run, I was shot down, captured and made a Prisoner of War.*

I began my incarceration in the infamous "Hanoi Hilton"–the name that POWs sarcastically gave to one of the worst prisoner camps in North Vietnam. We lived in solitary confinement in cramped, dirty cells. The cell windows were boarded up so that our only source of light came from cracks in the cell door and a huge, but very low-wattage, light bulb that hung from the middle of the ceiling. The summers were sweltering and the winters provided little relief. We suffered from dysentery, boils and heat rash, received no real medical attention, and were routinely interrogated, beaten and tortured. My friend and fellow POW John McCain pretty well summed up our experience in his book, *Faith of My Fathers,* when he described it as "organized inhumanity on a greater scale than [he] had conceived possible."**

In terms of how our culture defines "victims," I suppose most people would say that POWs fit the bill. Life was hard and our captors were vicious. We were ten thousand miles from home, sick or wounded, half-starved to death, and systematically abused by people who would have been just as happy to see us drop dead. But despite their best (and substantial) efforts, our captors could not get us to behave like victims–much to their enormous frustration. Frankly, had we done so, we would have been dead men. And I don't mean that metaphorically.

---

*Ever the humorist, my wife made me a jacket patch that reads "96½ Missions in Vietnam."

**John McCain and Mark Salter, *Faith of My Fathers* (New York: Random House, 1999), 253.

Pushing aside the countless things we could *not* do, my fellow POWs and I focused on whatever we could think of that we *could* do. If we were put in total isolation, a situation we knew created dangerous psychological strain, we devised mental strategies to get ourselves through it intact. When they brought out the tortures, we refused to give in to the fear or the pain. Instead, we became infuriated–lying, cheating, stealing–whatever it took to win a small victory over our captors. When they tried to isolate us by placing us in separate cells, we developed methods of communication using taps on the walls and flashed hand signals. In short, we took it upon ourselves to do whatever needed to be done to survive. Of those who lived to see freedom, many of us came away with life-long physical handicaps. But we mostly came through the better for our experience and, significantly, without bitterness or regret.

I attribute this success in large measure to the excellent preparation we received at the Naval Academy. The Academy knew, as we did, that capture was a possibility and they prepared us well for it. But I believe that it is also due, at least in part, to the fact that my buddies and I grew up in a time when kids were taught to expect difficulty in life. Bloody noses and bruised feelings were just a part of the game, and you learned early on how to roll with the punches.

Fast-forward a couple of decades, and everything seems to have turned 180 degrees. Most adults today appear hell-bent on shielding youngsters from experiencing discomfort. Schools have banned playground games like tag and dodge-ball; some sports leagues no longer keep score; and, evidently, somewhere along the line some well-meaning parents decided that everyone who plays on a sports team should get a trophy–win or lose, good player or poor. I'd be willing to bet that most of you reading this have several dozen trophies gathering dust on your shelves at home. They probably don't mean that much to you, do they? But, if any of you have a trophy that you won–really won–now that one means something! That one you can pick out of the crowd. It's a source of pride, and rightfully so.

The "feel-good" approach, however well-intentioned, has led to unintended consequences. Specifically, it has led many young people (and that includes many of you) to believe that they are *entitled* to feel happy and comfortable as they go through life. While it's great in theory to believe we should all be treated the same, be equally talented, and be equally lucky in what comes our way, life just isn't like that! And if you think that it is, you're in for a rough ride.

The good news is that you can, in fact, withstand *far* more discomfort and disappointment than you might imagine; and you can achieve far more success in life than you can even dream of right now. But you'll never achieve any of it if you cannot learn to embrace–or at least tolerate–failure and disappointment at some level. Nor will you succeed if you are in the habit of feeling sorry for yourself or if you are in the habit of expecting someone else to come in and make things better for you.

And so, contrary to the feel-good philosophy, here is what I hope for you: I hope that at some point you get pushed up against the wall so hard you're sure you can't recover, but somehow find a way to. I hope that you meet with obstacles so immense they stop you in your tracks, and you summon the strength to overcome them. I hope you experience the possibility of terrible failure and continue forward undaunted. In other words, what I hope for each of you is that, as you travel the road of life, you are given the opportunity to develop within yourself the tools you need to descend into the valleys and return again to the mountaintops.

Here is a little something to help you along your way. In no particular order, they are my "Rules for a Successful Life" (there is one for each year I was imprisoned, in case you're counting):

1. Stop dwelling on the negative. Exorcise phrases like "This is too hard!" and "That wasn't fair!" from your vocabulary. That kind of thinking gets you nowhere.

2. Bad things are going to happen. There's no way around it. When they do, work the problem. Don't whine about it. *Work the problem.* Simple.

3. (#3 is really a follow-up to #2) No matter how bad things seem, you can get through it. Don't look for sympathy because things are tough. Instead ask yourself, "What do I have to do to get out of this? What can I do to get back to where I want to be?" Don't wait around for somebody to come and help you.

4. Expect some failure: Part of learning what you are good at comes

from learning what you're *not* good at. If you really want to do something, do it. If you can't do it well, learn to do it better. Or better yet, figure out what you do *well* and keep doing that. Make that your signature. It takes some folks a little longer than others to figure out what that is. But it shows itself eventually.

5. Sometimes life is unfair. Okay, so now what? Either fix it or, if you can't fix it, learn to live with it or press on to something else. But don't lapse into self-pity because as soon as you do, as soon as you start feeling sorry for yourself, everything stops. You're through making progress. Remember, you are not a victim because of what happens to you. You *become* a victim by the way you respond to the events in your life.

6. Help the little guy. If someone weaker than you is getting picked on, you go help him out, *period*. There's not any moral equivalence here; you just go and break it up. Put a stop to it. You take the punches yourself if you have to.

7. No matter how bad you think you've got it, there is someone who has it worse. A lot worse.

Finally, if all else fails, remember this: *There's no such thing as a bad day when there's a doorknob on the inside of the door!*

Tim Reid

Tim Reid

Tim Reid is an award-winning actor, writer, director and producer whose work spans multiple generations and genres. Perhaps best known for his role as the iconic DJ "Venus Flytrap" on the long-running series *WKRP in Cincinnati*, Tim has written, starred in, and produced numerous acclaimed series, including *Simon & Simon, Amen, Snoops,* and the Emmy-award winning *Frank's Place,* one of the finest television programs ever to grace the small screen. Recently, Tim enjoyed lead and recurring roles on the hit television series *Sister, Sister* and *That '70s Show*.

He has been nominated multiple times for both Emmy and Golden Globe awards, and is the recipient of countless other awards, including an NAACP Image Award, a Critics Choice Award, and a Viewers for Quality Television Award. In 1999, he was honored by the Producers Guild of America with the prestigious Oscar Micheaux Award for outstanding lifetime achievement. The recipient of no less than six honorary degrees, Tim was inducted into the National Black College Hall of Fame in 1991. In 1998, he was named "Virginian of the Year" by the Virginia Press Association.

Tim is the founder of the annual Tim Reid Celebrity Weekend in Norfolk, Virginia, a charitable endeavor that has raised hundreds of thousands of dollars to help disadvantaged college students through the Virginia Scholarship and Youth Development Foundation. He also holds memberships in the Writers Guild of America and the Screen Actors Guild.

In 1997, Tim and his wife, actress Daphne Maxwell Reid, co-founded New Millennium Studios, a full-service film studio located in Petersburg, Virginia, dedicated to producing movies, documentaries and other programs that address important social issues through authentic portrayals of the broader African-American experience.

Editor's Note

I met with Tim Reid at his Petersburg, Virginia, office, which is located on the large parcel of land that houses New Millennium Studios, the television and film production company he founded with his wife, Daphne Maxwell Reid, in 1997. We talked for several hours about everything from world religion to racism. He was at times funny, intense, passionate and reserved. When we finally said good-bye, I felt exhausted—and secretly thrilled to have spent time with someone I had watched on television for so many years!

Far more than a resident funny-man, Tim Reid embodies the complexities of his work. He is as much "Venus Flytrap," the quick-witted, philosopher of the airwaves he portrayed on WKRP in Cincinnati, *as he is Frank Parrish, the struggling restaurateur he portrayed in the critically acclaimed series,* Frank's Place. *A fixture in Hollywood for more than 30 years, he has ridden the proverbial rollercoaster of fame through both the highs and the lows, and he has come away from that experience with a profound understanding both of fame's power and its limitations. His work in front of and behind the camera likewise has afforded him unique insights into the ways in which media can be, and often is, used to manipulate and influence public opinion. Thus, while he still enjoys acting, Tim currently devotes much of his time to producing films and television programs that provide authentic, uplifting portrayals of the broader African-American experience. This work, which reaches across cultures and generations, provides a potent and much-needed antidote to the tired, and often negative, portrayals of African-Americans in mainstream media.*

I am honored to introduce to you a man I believe to be one of the most gifted and innovative creative talents in American cinematic history, Mr. Tim Reid.

A Conversation with Tim Reid

KHJ: As you know, the point of this book is to pull together the wisdom and life stories of one generation to share with the next. The idea for the book was born from the fact that a lot of that information just doesn't seem to be getting passed along. Why is that, do you think? Why is it–or why does it seem–so much harder to pass along wisdom and life lessons to the next generation?

Tim: Why is it so hard for wisdom to get passed along today? That's easy: never has there been a media structure so powerful and so isolated in the hands of so few people, and propaganda so widely used–and misused–in a blatant attempt to control the behavior of people, than that which exists today. We went over to Iraq on a hunt for weapons of mass destruction when the most powerful man-made force in the world today is in our own backyard. Used improperly, the "weapon of mass destruction" is the media–and those who control it.

Information is broadcast in so many forms and on so many levels [nowadays], how can a person begin to distinguish the positive from the negative? And how can we expect a young mind that is being flooded with text messaging, iPods, and television–literally at every turn–to be still long enough to think and reflect on what they're being told by a parent or an elder? It is nearly impossible.

I was in Atlanta yesterday sitting in the CNN center with a young person, and we were talking about this very issue. Her solution was simply to tell people to turn their televisions off. I said, "Look around you!" and I pointed her to the big flat screen TV right next to us and the one next to it and the one next to it–there must have been 15 to 20 visual media going at the same time. And on each screen was the commercial about the caveman–"So easy a caveman could do it"–that the Martin Agency here in Richmond created. I asked her why she thought they were running that commercial, and she answered very logically, "Because they are trying to sell us something." That's *half*-true. But, as I told her, it's also there because they've shot a series based on these characters. So guess what?

You're going to be seeing a lot of these cavemen in the coming months because they want you to watch the series. They are *conditioning you to like the series*!

KHJ: *A series based on the cavemen. Seriously?*

Tim: Yep. And it's probably going to be a hit. I'm not saying whether it's good or bad—I don't know. I've never seen it. But I do know that the use of the media to *condition* you and your behavior is pervasive. It's calculated. And it is effective! That's what people do, you know? I mean, when you only have five or six companies controlling 80 percent of all the media in the world, and they want to sell you something, why wouldn't they use it? You can't even get on the elevator in any media building in New York where there isn't a TV screen. The media is constantly feeding you—bombarding you—with social behavior conditioning. So, when you tell a young kid, "Don't sell drugs! Don't buy those rims! Don't waste money! Think beyond the now!"—well, look what the media (and not just television—all media), look what it's telling them: "You *want* these rims! You *need* all these gadgets! You've got to have a *style!*"

So, consequently, it's difficult—more difficult than ever—to get young men and women to accept wisdom from an elder or wisdom from a parent. [They question] whether what we have to say *is* wisdom any more. Of course, those of us who have the information know that it is; but how do you tell them and then show them examples? You don't control the media and almost every example they're seeing is *counter to [what you're telling them]*.

KHJ: *I think, too, this generation—raised on computers, BlackBerries and downloads—they see the media as their friend. Even if they have a sense they're being marketed to, they see it all as basically friendly. And the people in charge know that. They count on it and they cultivate that "relationship."*

Tim: Of course they do! The people who control the media are intelligent—no doubt about it. But they are intelligent in ways that come from the use of things to create wealth—not in creating a better culture or better society.

I used to be a very conspiratorial-minded person. But the deeper I've gotten into [television and film] production—and especially when I built my studio a few years ago—the more I've realized that I gave these people too much credit. There is no cabal somewhere saying, "We will take their minds and make them believe in our philosophy!" Huh-uh. These people are simply in the business of creating wealth. Their theory—and in time we will find out if they are right or wrong—is that through wealth the world can be changed. There is not a problem that these people believe can't be solved by money! So consequently they don't see the value of interaction or social behavior. They don't pay any attention to that. What drives them is using information, or rather, using the *control* of information, to create enormous wealth. And they have succeeded. So again, looking at it from this point of view, I think to tell young people, "Don't watch! Cut back on this! Cut back on that!" is a waste of time.

KHJ: *I agree.*

Tim: Here is a perfect, real-life story that illustrates the point better than any admonition ever could. I was talking with a young woman a while back—a celebrity who had come down to a fundraising event I was attending. We were talking and she said that her son—six years old I believe—had almost drowned in their pool at home. She can't swim and so, when he fell in, she stood by the side of the pool not knowing what to do. Well, she finally jumped in after him and she fought and struggled and somehow—as mothers can do—got herself to a point where she could touch bottom. She was so frightened having almost lost her son and her own life! When I asked her what she'd done in response to this event, she told me she had built a fence around the pool. And I thought, "Well, that is a modern way to approach the problem! But, why not teach your kid to swim?"

She wanted an easy solution—a *money* solution. But the fact remains that anybody who owns a swimming pool and can't swim is stupid! (laughs) Anyone who lives near the ocean and can't swim is stupid. Move inland! That doesn't mean people who can swim don't sometimes drown, but it certainly improves your odds!

KHJ: *That reminds me of the old* Jaws *movies—"Hello? Stop going back into the water!"*

Tim: Yeah—exactly! So, to me, this is a perfect example of what is going on in our culture. When I tell young men the story about the woman and the pool they say, "Of *course* she should [learn to swim]! If you live near the ocean or you own a pool, you should know how to swim!" Well, the pool in our case is the flood of information from the media. Young people can't get away from it—no one can get away from it! But what I try to get across to them is the fact that they have got to learn to be *smart* with the information. They've got to think!

KHJ: *That flood of information is so well-packaged. It is terribly compelling—podcasts, downloads, high-tech graphics . . .*

Tim: Oh, absolutely. It draws us in—all of us. Our culture has an insatiable appetite for media—especially pop-culture media. I mean, just look who our icons are—that tells you a lot about society. Our icons are people like Anna Nicole Smith (more popular dead than alive) and Paris Hilton. Paris Hilton comes from a wealthy family. She can't act, can't sing, and she's had sex with people on video. So, what makes her an icon? The *media*. The media builds these things. They build them, they destroy them, they build them, they destroy them. But they create them.

In the novel *Brave New World*, Aldous Huxley warned that the fear of mankind should be that we live in a world of *perception* and not reality. Why? Because you cannot build a defense against perception. Young people today—and in fact anyone who is hypnotized by the power of the media—live in a world of *perception*. And the perception, as I said earlier, is that money can fix *anything*. If you go out and look at what we're fed every day by the media, that one idea is the most persistent. "Money is the answer to all our ills, globally and personally!" That is ridiculous. And it is not only ridiculous, it is impossible!

KHJ: *But people do need money to get by. So, isn't there an argument to be made that money is the answer—at least to some degree?*

Tim: Not money—*prosperity!* We need *prosperity*. Everyone has a right to be prosperous: have a decent education, a decent home, healthcare, all those things. These are the elements of a good community and society. But many people make the mistake of thinking wealth and prosperity are the same thing. Prosperity and money or prosperity and wealth are *two different things*. So, the *reality* is we have a right to be prosperous. But the *perception*, handed to us by the media, is that we need to be rich.

KHJ: *Let's talk about role models for a moment. You used the word elders a minute ago—that's a great word. Role models used to be elders—grown men, fathers, uncles—people who had life experience and some knowledge to pass along. Now, "role models" are typically artists who are the same age or maybe a few years older than our readers. There's an element to that that feels like the blind leading the blind.*

Tim: Role models today are anybody who makes money. And most young people don't even care how [the person they admire] made it. All they see is that he or she has made *a lot* of money. I want to be clear–I'm not against people making money. I don't care how much money someone makes. But I *do* care when they seem to lack a purpose. You can have all the money in the world, but if you don't have a purpose . . . well, that's where the evil lies. That's where the darkness is.

Let's imagine you're a young person and you go out and get all this wealth– what's your purpose? What are you going to do with it? Are you going to enrich your life and the lives of others? Or are you just going to be rich?

KHJ: *Switching gears slightly, what is your take on the controversy surrounding the use of "offensive" language in rap music?*

Tim: Frankly, I disagree. I refuse to go along with censorship of words. I don't think we should stop them from saying the N word, the B word, the H word–I'm against that. And the reason I'm against it is because it's like the woman with the pool. Teach them to swim! Teach them the concept of responsibility! Taking words away from them–they're just going to find other words.

I was talking to some of the guys in the music industry just this weekend and I told them, you keep saying those words and this is what's going to happen. Warner Brothers records and Universal–they're getting a lot of flack because they're looking bad. Pretty soon, some college trust fund is going to say, "We're selling this stock because you're putting out filth!" That's going to hit the stock market, and I'm going to be watching CNBC one evening, and Time Warner stock is going to drop by three or four points. Well, that's the equivalent of hundreds of millions of dollars! That happens two or three days in a row, and somebody [in charge] is going to call the record company and say, "Don't put out another record like that!"– and hang up. Then, the next time rappers bring in their stuff, they're going to hear, "Sorry, we're not buying that anymore. It makes us look bad."

This situation is going to last for awhile, and during that time, those artists are dead in the water. They don't get the rims, they don't get the car, they don't get any of it. Dead in the water. And this is what I try to tell them—that by using this language, they're killing the business, and they need to think about that and take responsibility. *That's* why you stop using those words. That's why. And that is how the next big creative leap takes place. I guarantee you, the next big innovation in music will rise out of those ashes.

KHJ: If people could get behind the Hollywood glamour and get a bird's eye view into the lives of movie stars, television stars, etc., what would they be shocked to discover?

Tim: Oh, that's simple—how afraid they are. There is so much fear in Hollywood among celebrities; there is a pure, unadulterated fear that permeates that community. I felt it [myself] before I came here. People in Hollywood are driven by fear—they can't sleep without drugs, they're haunted by a fear of losing, fear of not being accepted, of not getting a job. Fear is the constant, motivating force. You're ruled by it and, if you're lucky enough to rise to the top, you rule with it. If young people really understood how afraid folks are in Hollywood (and in politics and executive board rooms, for that matter) they would be shocked!

KHJ: What would you say was one of the defining moments of your life—a time when you either did "the right thing" or failed to do the right thing and learned from it?

Tim: There have been several defining moments, but the one that jumps to mind is this. It begins with something my father taught me. He always said, "You've got to respect truth and brute force." What does that mean? It means this: I don't care how intelligent you are, if you're in a situation and you see someone has lost control of his human faculties and is ready to resort to brute force, you'd better be ready (1) to take that person out or (2) do whatever it is you need to do to protect yourself. You've got to be wise enough to know when things have gone too far and tell yourself, *in the moment*, "I either need to back up, attack, or whatever." But you'd better be keeping your eye on the ball.

Now, when I was at the top of my game in Hollywood—in control, in demand, and in a position to make demands, creating wealth for myself and the system—I had a show I had produced, created, written, and starred in called *Snoops*. While I was working on *Snoops*, I did a favor for an executive over at the network. I took this guy—a hard-headed guy—off his hands. [This executive] did not want to fire him because the guy's father was extremely important in the industry, so I agreed to let him come and work for me on the show. I knew the guy was a tyrant, but I didn't really care because this was my show and I was in charge. But what I didn't see was that he was very, very sneaky. Without my knowing it, he was going behind my back and doing and saying things to undermine my power and responsibility with the network. A few episodes into the series, he got so full of himself that he failed to do his job–failed to get the set ready for a shoot.

In this particular case, I was the boss. He worked for me. So I went in and said to him, "Young man, you're not doing your job." Now, you want to see some sparks fly–you let a black man tell a white man he's not being professional! (laughs) Well, he was certainly insulted and he said something back that was insulting–not racial–this was not a racial thing. This was basically two alpha males fighting for control of the pack. But in that alpha-maleness there is a certain ignorance that is sort of built-in, and when you "lose it," you forget to keep your eye on the ball. And that day I forgot that his father was one of the most powerful people in Hollywood. In a sense–brute force. And I fired him.

Well, my lawyers and my people called me saying, "Don't do this! You do *not* want to do this!" But by then I was adamant. It had reached a point where I felt my integrity and my alpha-maleness were at stake and then, to me, it became racial. *I* made it racial because, in my mind, in my thinking, I'm back in the civil rights era, I'm back in Norfolk during segregation. I'm thinking, "This man was wrong. This is my show. If I want him gone, he's gone." Everybody said, "Don't do it," . . . and I didn't listen. And it hurt my career, [and still does] in many ways, to this day. That *one* incident.

I left Hollywood after that, moved to Virginia and eventually built this studio. I decided to produce films on my own so that if I failed, I was going to fail by my own hand. And I have not really been involved with Hollywood since.

KHJ: If you could have played it differently, would you?

Tim: I would have played it wiser. I would have approached him and presented him with his inadequacies and with the fact that he was not doing his job. But I would have gone through the chain of command and let other people take it through the regular channels. I would have done it without using my power or my alpha-maleness to the ultimate end—my own destruction.

I had the power to fire him, so the fact that I fired him was not the issue. It was *how* it was done. My ego got into it and I forgot the lesson my father had handed down to me. In life, you are going to find yourself in situations where you must determine whether this is the time, whether this is the fight you must fight. Every person will face that challenge. And you have to have the wisdom to pick the right battle. If you pick that battle at the right time, you'll be immortal. You'll be a hero. But if you don't, it could be the thing that destroys you and that you may never recover from. Look at Tupac [Shakur]*—what a future he would have had! But like *he* said, "I picked the wrong battle. I didn't get the information." There were no elders around him!

KHJ*: We're back to elders. We've come full circle. Before I go, will you be so kind as to indulge me in a little word association?*

Tim: Go ahead.

KHJ*: Compassion.*

Tim: Love.

KHJ*: Bullies.*

Tim: Dead.

KHJ*: Boys don't cry.*

Tim: Bullshit.

KHJ*: Respect for women*

Tim: Paramount.

---

*Tupac Shakur, a superstar rap artist whose edgy lyrics gave voice to both the violence of inner city and the need for social justice, was murdered in a drive-by shooting in Las Vegas. He was 25 years old.

Matt Hasselbeck

Matt Hasselbeck

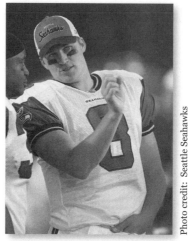

Photo credit: Seattle Seahawks

Matt Hasselbeck is the starting quarterback for the NFL's Seattle Seahawks. Originally drafted by the Green Bay Packers out of Boston College in 1998, he spent two seasons as the back-up quarterback to Brett Favre. In 1999, then-Packers head coach Mike Holmgren left Green Bay to take the head coaching job at Seattle. Two years later, Holmgren, famous for having trained quarterbacks Joe Montana, Steve Young and Brett Favre, hand-picked Matt to be the starting quarterback for the Seahawks and arranged a trade with the Packers to bring him onboard.

Holmgren's eye for talent proved to be prescient once again as Matt's career began to flourish in Seattle. Since his arrival in 2001, Matt has led the Seahawks to four consecutive division titles and five consecutive play-off appearances. Following a stellar season in 2005, Matt helped the Seahawks make their first trip to the Super Bowl in the team's 30-year history.

Matt was selected to the Pro Bowl three times, was named All Pro in 2005, and holds the title as the all-time, highest-rated passer ever to play for the Seahawks franchise. Along the way, he has received numerous honors and awards including the *Seattle Post-Intelligencer* Sports Star of the Year, the FedEx Air Player of the Week (twice), the NFC Offensive Player of the Month and the NFC Offensive Player of the Week.

Editor's Note

Ask just about anyone who follows professional football about Matt Hasselbeck, and I bet you 10 to 1 that one of the first things they'll tell you is, "He's a great guy." At least this is what I had heard about a thousand times before I met him. And now I know why. He is one of the nicest and most down-to-earth people I've ever had the pleasure to interview. He is also a huge Celtics fan, something he put to good comical use the day I met him.

I had arranged to talk with him on what turned out to be a ridiculously cold June day at the Seahawks office in Kirkland, Washington. He walked off the elevator wearing a Celtics jersey and a look that said he was up to something. "Can you hang on just a sec?" he asked, then walked over and stood in front of one of the offices that lined the hallway, flaunting his Boston green and pointing to the now captive gentleman inside. I couldn't hear the man's response, but whatever it was, it made Matt laugh out loud. "Sorry about that," he said as he walked back to start the interview. "He's a big Lakers fan, so I'm obligated to give him some grief." Before I could respond, his hand was outstretched toward mine. "Hi, I'm Matt," he said with a smile. "It's nice to meet you."

And so I am delighted to present my interview with one of the true good guys of the NFL, Mr. Matt Hasselbeck.

A Conversation with Matt Hasselbeck

KHJ: If I asked you to tell me about one of the greatest men you know—or know of—who would that be?

Matt: I feel really fortunate—I feel like I can pick from a lot of people. I know some of my friends feel like they could name only one or two people; and there are some who don't feel they could name any. But, I'd choose my dad. He'd be my first choice.

KHJ: Why?

Matt: I had a great childhood growing up, and that is because of both my mom and my dad. But as a boy, you know, you want to grow up and be like your father. I remember that people would always ask me what I wanted to do when I grew up, and I didn't have any idea. But I would always say, "Oh, I don't know. I guess I'll just play in the NFL like my dad."* Of course when I said that, I'd probably never even played football! (laughs) But growing up, I always admired my dad. He and my mom were very, very strict; but they lived what they taught me and my brothers. It was never, "Do what I say, not what I do." He really lived it.

But even though he was strict, we had a lot of fun growing up. My parents were young when they had me and so, in some ways, it was like a friendship at times. The funny thing is that, as I grew older, I started hearing all these stories about [my dad] from guys that he had gone to high school with or college with—or even guys that he played with early on in his NFL career. And the version of him, the man that they described—I never met that guy.

---

*Matt's father, Don Hasselbeck, is a former NFL tight end. He was originally drafted in 1977 by the New England Patriots, where he played for seven seasons, before moving on to play for the Los Angeles Raiders, the Minnesota Vikings, and the New York Giants. He retired from professional football in 1985.

KHJ: *What was so different?*

Matt: Well, he grew up being a star athlete and kind of a tough guy. Apparently he had a short temper and got into fights in high school. He'd get kicked out of a game for yanking the ref's whistle—you know, crazy things. (laughs) In the very first NFL game he ever played in—with the New England Patriots—he ran down to cover a kick-off and he got into a fight. I think it was against their archrival, the New York Jets. Anyway, all of the Patriots fans are giving him a standing ovation as he's getting a police escort off the field! So he was just a very tough, hard-nosed football player—and that never changed. But *he* changed. Somewhere during, I'd say, the early 1980s, he really grew as a person.

KHJ: *What do you think changed him?*

Matt: I think it was his faith. Even though he grew up going to church, I believe that his faith became real to him around that time, and he started to live according to what his faith said. That was around second or third grade for me, so that's the guy I remember. I just remember the really awesome version of him.

KHJ: *That's incredibly admirable because, in my experience, most people who grow up having a temper never find a way to really overcome it. It takes an iron will and incredible self-control to decide, "Hey, I'm not going to act that way anymore."*

Matt: Absolutely. But you know, that is the kind of guy he is. He was, still is, to this day, a bit of a survivor. If tough stuff gets thrown his way, he just does what it takes to get through. He's a problem solver. I can remember times when he was stuck behind an All-Pro player and didn't get a chance to really show what he had to offer on the field or he got traded or they said he was too old to be playing—whatever it was, he would push forward. He did what he had to do and he handled it the right way. He just had a lot of perseverance and the determination to make it work. I think he brought that same determination to his own life and turned things around.

KHJ: *He sounds like a great guy . . . which, of course, is something I hear said about you all the time. Everyone I talk to, everything I read, it seems, describes you as being "a great guy." That's the mantra. I'm curious why you think it is that people say that about you.*

Matt: I don't know if everyone would say that! (laughs) I know what I think of as a great guy. But people throw that phrase around like it's nothing: "Oh yeah, he's a great guy." And whether they are saying it about me or someone else, I usually correct them. I say, "He's a *good* guy." Nothing against whoever they're talking about. But if you're going to say someone's a *great* guy.... There are only a couple of men I know who are great guys: Jim Zorn, Danny Wuerffel, my dad, maybe one or two more.

KHJ: *Interesting. So what makes someone "great"?*

Matt: For me, I feel like the guys I would put in that category are people who legitimately will put others first. That's a very hard thing to do. I just don't think most people are that way. I don't think *I'm* that way.

KHJ: *Okay, then tell me about one of these gentlemen you mentioned. Jim Zorn,* for example. What do you see Jim Zorn do (or not do) that makes him one of those "great" men?*

Matt: On a daily basis, a *daily* basis—he is a guy who is not at all concerned with who gets the credit. And, if he's concerned about it, then it's because he wants others to get the credit he thinks they deserve. He's the first person to say, "Hey that's a great job," about someone else; or, if something goes bad, he's the first guy to say, "That's my fault." He's doing that and he's the *coach*—he *was* my coach. Another thing—typically, the coach tells players what to do. Not the case with him. He'd be the guy "serving" us. He'd be the one asking, "What do you need? What can I do for you?" He'd be carrying water bottles out or, if we needed a bag of footballs to throw at practice—the rookies aren't carrying that bag; the back-up's not carrying that bag; I'm not carrying that bag. He's carrying it! He was just the guy who did everything the opposite of what you would expect.

KHJ: *Why does he do that, do you think? I mean, you talked about him carrying the bag of footballs for his players, and I can't help contrast that with a picture I saw a few years back of a well-known rapper*

---

*Jim Zorn was the Seattle Seahawks expansion team's first quarterback, playing from the team's inception in 1976 through the 1984 season. He is one of only eight people to have been inducted into the Seahawks Ring of Honor. Since his retirement from professional football, he has coached at both the collegiate and professional levels, notably as quarterback coach for the Seahawks from 2001-2007. In February 2008, he was named head coach of the Washington Redskins.

who decided it was a good idea to employ another human being as his "personal umbrella holder"—something that seemed to me so ridiculous it bordered on obscene. But the media ate it up, and it cemented his reputation as some kind of superstar. So, there's a very real pay-off in our culture for self-glorifying behavior. And I am left wondering what the "pay-off" is for men like Jim Zorn? What does he know that we have perhaps lost sight of?

Matt: My guess is that it goes back to his faith, his Christian faith and modeling what Jesus taught. But you don't need to be a Christian or even believe in that to understand what he is doing. If I were going to try to explain what he stands for to someone, I would use this example: There are people—just like you said—there are people who, when they walk into a room, it's basically, "Hey, look at *me*." But with Jim—and guys like him—he walks into a room and it's, "Hey, look at *you*." And in the context of being on a football team, it's refreshing when you have someone who is that way because when you're with people all the time, day-in-and-day-out, through good and bad, you see their true colors. In our game there are times when it's tough; it's physical, you have injuries, and you can find yourself facing huge "mountains," if you will. When that happens, who do you want to be with? You want to be with the kind of people who you can trust and who you can count on to help build you up. Not break you down for their own gain.

Jim Zorn did that; and it made you want to be the best player you could be for him.

KHJ: *So what do you say to young men who may want to aspire to that measure of "greatness"? Where do they begin?*

Matt: I say, accept the risk of being a leader. Because it *is* a risk—you're putting yourself out there. Being a leader isn't about going with the grain. It's about ignoring what's popular and doing what's right. And nothing about that is easy. It's not easy to stand up to a group of your friends and say something like, "Hey, why are you smoking? That's not cool." It's not easy to say you're not going to cheat when people ask you to or you see them doing it. But I'd rather have an honest "C+" than an "A" I got by cheating. Those things aren't what's popular; but that's being a leader, in my opinion. When I go out and talk to young guys, especially young quarterbacks, I've really tried to share with them how those things that happen off the football field carry over onto the field. That skill set, and the fact that you're choosing to act with integrity all the time–it matters. Your teammates see it and, as a quarterback, you need to be that guy in that huddle they know for sure: They know who you are, they know where you stand, they know what you stand for.

KHJ: *Those qualities sound to me like they would apply to anyone who is interested in being a leader, whether they play football or not. It's just a good, sound definition of leadership.*

Matt: Probably. But I don't know if I'm old enough to be giving life lessons or saying what's right for everybody. I try to stick to what I know, and what I know for sure is what it is like to be a high school quarterback. I know the pressures. I know the temptations. I know the opportunities.

KHJ: *Tell me about 15- or 16-year-old Matt Hasselbeck.*

Matt: Young and with a whole lot more hair! But seriously, I guess I was a kid with a lot of potential and a lot was expected of me. But I had not really filled into my body at all, and I was trying–as a sophomore and a junior–to lead juniors and seniors who were bigger than me, older than me, tougher than me. They were from the city. I was from a little bit of a sheltered, maybe a little bit pampered, background. The first job of a quarterback is to step into the huddle and take command–you're the only guy who speaks and everyone's looking at you. But I had to step into the huddle before I was really ready. I'd be coming into a game where all these guys had these dirty uniforms–they've got dirty, muddy uniforms on–and I walk out in my brand-spanking new, white uniform!

KHJ: *Oh jeez!*

Matt: "Oh jeez" is right!

KHJ: *What was one of the toughest moments in all that for you?*

Matt: I think it was my sophomore year. None of the upperclassmen really liked me–or maybe they wanted to toughen me up–so they put something like a bounty on my head so that whoever hit me the hardest or hurt me at training camp got some money.

KHJ: *Are you kidding me?*

Matt: (laughs) That's just the nature of growing up in Boston. Things like that happen. But yeah, it's tough. It's tough and you've got to grow up fast.

KHJ: *What did you take away from that?*

Matt: That quitting wasn't an option. There were so many times I wanted to quit, but it just was not an option. So you just make it work; you survive it. Obviously you've got to be physically tough, but being mentally tough is so important.

I also knew I had to earn their respect. There are a couple of ways to do that in football: one is to work hard and two is to perform well. Fortunately, the two usually go hand in hand. So I tried to work hard and perform well; and each day, I would maybe win over one guy. The next day I'd win over another guy and slowly, it came together.

KHJ: *If you could go back in time and give your 16- or 17-year-old self some advice, what would it be?*

Matt: I don't know. I don't know what I'd say because I wouldn't want to change too much. Even through the bad stuff I learned a lot and grew a lot. If I were to say anything, it would be, "Don't do anything that the 32-year-old you would be disappointed in." I don't think I did, but I wouldn't have come so close from time to time.

KHJ: *We'll end with a little word association, if that's okay.*

Matt: Sure.

KHJ: *Compassion.*

Matt: Mother Teresa.

KHJ: *Respect for women.*

Matt: Essential.

KHJ: *Bullies.*

Matt: Scared.

KHJ: *Boys don't cry.*

Matt: *Not* true.

Kevin Smith

Kevin Smith

Photo credit: Smith family

Kevin Smith is a youth counselor who has a gift for working with young people facing life's enormous challenges, from troubled boys living in group homes to the young men and women incarcerated at San Diego's Juvenile Hall. A counselor for more than 16 years, Kevin most recently brought his unique talents to a high school in San Diego where he works to help students find their way to personal, academic and social success.

Kevin holds a B.A. in behavioral science, an M.S. in educational counseling, and an M.S. in school psychology. In 2001, he was one of eight educators selected to participate in a forum on the problem of alcohol, tobacco and drug use in schools with Bill Modzeleski, then director of the Safe and Drug-Free Schools and Communities Program at the United States Department of Education. In February 2008, he was recognized by the National Sorority of Phi Delta Kappa Inc., Delta Upsilon Chapter, as "Outstanding African American Educator."

Kevin has written and produced five anti-gang/pro-education videos, and has been interviewed on numerous local television and radio programs. A sought-after speaker, he appears regularly at youth retreats, parent education seminars and at student assemblies in both public and private schools.

Editor's Note

For some folks, childhood is blissful. For others, it is a time to which they are grateful never to have to return. After all, kids can be brutal to one another, and it doesn't matter that they are "only" eight or eleven or thirteen; some real, lasting damage can be done.

I wish I could tell you that getting over these childhood hurts just "happens" as you get older. But the truth is that unexamined pain behaves much like an untreated wound. It festers and scars. And because wading through all that old hurt is so damn hard to do, few of us make the effort. So, somewhere in the back of our minds lives that kid who was picked on, or unpopular, or neglected, or otherwise made to feel "less than." And he intrudes on our lives—whether we know it or not.

Kevin Smith is not like most people, however. He was a late bloomer and, like many late bloomers, he had a terrible time fitting in. As a result, his middle and high school years are made up of mostly painful memories. Eventually he grew up, of course; and, from all outward appearances, seemed to be making his way in the world. Inside, however, Kevin Smith was seething. His pain had turned into anger that he could barely contain; and that is when Kevin did something extraordinary: he healed the wounds of his childhood.

It took time, extraordinary courage, and determination to do it, but he found a way. He found a way to let go of the angry, wounded boy still living inside him, and step forward into a life he would forge for himself, into the shoes of the man he wanted to be.

Kevin has spent the last decade or so trying to help some of the country's toughest, most vulnerable kids make the same leap. He has kindly agreed to share some of what he has learned, both about anger and how to heal it, here in this book. Oddly enough, his prescription for overcoming anger begins with killing . . . the spider.

I'm honored to introduce one of the most genuine and compassionate people I know, Mr. Kevin Smith.

Killing the Spider*

As I entered the maximum security unit in juvenile hall, I was overcome with excitement, anticipation and fear. Although I had been here many times before to talk to young men who had committed serious crimes, this case was different. The media frenzy that surrounded it, and the outrage people around the county felt at yet another innocent person falling victim to gang violence, had reached a level that prior cases had failed to achieve. People from all walks of life had eagerly awaited news from the police that they had apprehended the heartless monster responsible for this violent murder. This "heartless monster" was the young man I had come to meet.

I walked into the unit and let the probation officer know that I was there. I was shocked when he led me down the hall toward a small, almost frail, young boy being escorted by an enormous, Samoan police officer. "Kevin," he said to me, "this is Tom. You need the room?" I tried to sound as relaxed as possible. "Yeah," I told him, "the room is cool." Truthfully, pride alone prevented me from asking Tom's heavily-muscled police escort to stand close by when we walked into the small room within the heavily secured unit. In my mind, I rehearsed the self-defense moves I would perform if I was attacked by this killer kid.

I sat down and began giving Tom my normal spiel for newcomers: "My name is Kevin. I'm a counselor and I work for the school inside juvenile hall. I'm here to see where you are in school and how we can help you continue your education." Then, when my "recording" was over, I spoke from the heart. I explained to him that, while I knew he had more on his mind than school, I also knew from experience that focusing on school would give his mind something to think about other than his trial.

Contrary to the picture painted by the news media, Tom was soft-spoken, respectful, nonaggressive and very intelligent. It wasn't long before we

---

*Each of the men mentioned in this essay is a real person. However, their names have been changed to protect their privacy.

were able to talk comfortably with each other. I continued to meet with him throughout the weeks and months leading up to his trial. Because of my position within the legal system, I was constrained from talking with him about what happened the night of the murder. Regardless, we quickly developed a close bond. I knew and understood his situation and, in turn, he knew that while I had a job to do, I cared about him. Many days I drove home in silence thinking about what was going to happen to this young man. I concluded that either Tom deserved an Oscar for fine acting or that something had gone terribly wrong in his life.

After months of waiting, Tom's case finally came to trial. The courtroom was packed with family members, lawyers, news cameras and reporters. Wiping tears from his face, Tom shocked the prosecutor and the community by confessing that he had, in fact, pulled the trigger that had killed the young college student about to be married. Tom's grandfather, to whom he was very close, was barely able to prevent his tears from flowing in front of his grandson, but his quivering lip revealed the intense sadness he was feeling for the boy he loved so much. I mourned for the victim and his family–and for Tom.

In the end, the judge handed down a sentence of 25 years to life in prison. Tom was 14 years old.

After the sentencing, and with Tom's permission, his grandfather began telling Tom's story to students around the nation. The root of Tom's problem it seemed was a familiar foe to many. A childhood filled with more than his fair share of pain had left Tom consumed by anger. Much of that anger was justified; but Tom had never been given any tools to deal with it in a way that could have provided him with the healing he needed to move forward. As I thought about Tom and about how events in his life had brought him to such a tragic end, I couldn't help but think about my own life's journey. I remembered a statement I had heard years before–a statement that had changed the way I faced my own anger and now help teens overcome theirs: *"Stop wasting your time fighting cobwebs; kill the spider."*

I've heard this statement communicated in different ways over the years and, while the details can vary, the basic premise remains the same. The statement is part of a story that begins when a man goes into his basement and walks smack into an enormous cobweb. The man struggles to remove the cotton candy-like substance from his hair, face and body. Finally freed of the cobweb, the man goes back into his comfortable house feeling angry and frustrated. The next day he walks back into his basement and has the exact same experience. He shouts at the cobwebs that blanket his face and clothes as he begins the painstaking task of removing them a second time. When he has finally cleared all traces of the cobweb, he goes back into his house, twice as upset as before. The man continues this cycle until one day he realizes that if he dealt with the source of the cobwebs–the spider–he could put an end to his misery.

I spent a lot of my youth and young adulthood fighting cobwebs. My memories are riddled with incidents of uncontrolled anger, many of which have left me with deep regrets to this day. One of my most painful memories involves an incident that took place during my senior year in high school. There were two individuals on the school bus who harassed me nonstop. They routinely made fun of the low-level classes I was taking as a senior; they said I was too dumb to graduate; and, they seemed to take pleasure in letting me know that no one on the bus liked me. I tried to mask my anger, but the day finally came when it overwhelmed me. I physically assaulted them, leaving them severely, perhaps permanently, scarred. It was an incredible act of cowardice on my part considering that both of the individuals in question were girls. But, like trying to put toothpaste back in the tube after it's out, I could not undo the damage I had caused. I immediately wanted to comfort them in their pain and tell them how sorry I was for harming them. My youthful pride prevented me from doing so.

The truth was I didn't feel intelligent. When it came to brain power and common sense I had always felt like I'd missed the boat. It was as though everyone in the world had attended some meeting about how to succeed in life–and I'd been absent. These feelings caused me tremendous pain at the time. If that weren't enough, I also felt unattractive and unpopular. I'd always wanted to be the guy with the bulging legs and upper-body, and I did everything I could think of to add size to my painfully thin frame. I imitated the fictional boxer Rocky Balboa by drinking raw eggs (which I'm sure only raised my cholesterol level). I curled my barbell set countless times and ate peanut butter and banana sandwiches (only to have my physical education teacher say in front of the class that I shouldn't turn sideways because no one would see me). Nothing seemed to make any difference.

The harsh words coming from the girls on the bus that day only reminded me of how frustrated I was with myself. Their attitude towards me intensified my feelings of rejection from other pretty girls. When I lashed out in anger at them, it was my attempt to silence the voices that haunted me day and night as a teen; voices that told me that I was stupid, unattractive and of little worth.

As awful as this event was, however, it was not enough to motivate me to confront the unknown, internal enemies responsible for my torment. Instead, after I graduated from high school, I joined the U.S. Navy, certain that a geographical change could bring about an internal one. But I would soon discover that no matter how far I traveled, my spiders stayed with me. Because I had done poorly on the naval entrance exam, I was assigned a job in which I had little interest. It was hard, dirty work and the hours were long. Many of my shipmates considered my job to be the bottom of the barrel, which it was. This only added to my sense of frustration.

Throughout my time in the Navy, my lack of confidence in my intellectual abilities kept me from chasing my dreams and left me stuck in jobs that did not bring me any fulfillment. Time and again, I allowed anger to rule my interactions. I recall one occasion when my anger and frustration got the better of me and I got into a fight with one of my shipmates during a very dangerous ship operation. This was a turning point for me and, not long after, I made some decisions that would change my life forever.

Looking back now, in addition to being frightened by the fact that my anger had almost cost me my life and the lives of other sailors, I think that I was also just plain sick and tired of the way I was living–battling anger and frustration day after day after day. My problems had followed me wherever I went and, frankly, I was exhausted. I decided it was time for me to seek out the spiders in my life and deal with them head on. I was through with just clearing out the cobwebs.

I started by taking a long, solo drive to the mountains. Equipped with a notebook, pen and pencils, and a mini-recorder, I was ready to do business. I spent hours on that mountain examining my life, trying to determine what was responsible for my violent outbursts of anger. I made a long list of things that frustrated me. It didn't take long for me to see that all of the things on the list could be traced back to two things: (1) low self-esteem and (2) an intense desire to be accepted. These were my spiders. Once I had identified them, I began devising a plan to remove them from my life.

To raise my self-esteem, I committed myself to doing something I had never done seriously in high school—I studied! I began using the resources in the library in a consistent way for the first time in my life, and I discovered that I loved it! A few months later, I felt confident enough to enroll in college in hopes of rising above the minimum wage jobs I was so accustomed to by then. As for my physical appearance, I continued to exercise and take care of myself, but I accepted the fact that my body-type and metabolism would make it very difficult for me to make any major changes in my weight. Accepting the fact that the title "Big Man" was never going to be used to describe me was difficult. But in time, I made friends with my image. Last, and maybe most important, I accepted the fact that no matter what I did to improve myself, there would always be people who would not like me. (Though I admit that this last one still poses a challenge for me at times, as it does for many people.)

Throughout the years that followed, I kept the notes I had made during my time of self-discovery on the mountain close at hand. As I worked to "kill my spiders," my life was transformed. I not only graduated from college, but went on to earn a master's degree. In fact, as I write this, I am only three units shy of a second master's. I've been able to experience the joy of watching my home being built and, unlike my military career, I am in a job that both challenges and fulfills me. On the fun side, I no longer disappear when I stand sideways. These days I stand 6'1" and weigh 220 pounds. I've been called "Big Man" numerous times, but it doesn't bring me the satisfaction I thought it would years before. Making peace with the things I couldn't change about myself freed me from the vice-like grip anger once had on my life. Finally, I was able to experience the contentment that had eluded me for so long.

In 1996, I left my position at juvenile hall and went to work at Montgomery Middle School. It was there that I started an anger management class for students that I called "The Spider Patrol." All of the students in my class were one or two referrals away from being permanently expelled. Many were gang members, taggers, ditchers and drug users. "The Spider Patrol" became a safe place for all of us to share our stories with each other.

Months after the group began, I took the kids on a day trip to a nearby prison to participate in C.R.O.P (Convicts Reaching Out to People)—a program that allows students from around the county to spend the morning with selected prisoners, most of whom are "lifers"—men who have been sentenced to spend the remainder of their days in prison. Hearing these tattooed, hardened men share their stories and talk about the unresolved pain in their lives impacted all of us. I will never forget one man in particular, Peter A., who performed a powerful rap about all the regrets, pain and losses he had suffered. Peter is one of those men who, had he been in a different situation growing up, could have been a celebrity. I also had the opportunity to introduce my students to Sam G. and Greg M.–both ex-cons who have become role models for the kids I teach. Sam is part of a group of ex-cons who give back to their communities by helping students identify and overcome their pain. Greg is both a good personal friend and a former member of one of our country's most notorious gangs. Through his faith and with the help of friends, he left the gang life and later became a scholar, graduating cum laude from one of California's top universities. All three men set an extraordinary example, not for what they did in the past, but for what they are choosing to do with their pain! They have found ways to recycle it into something positive by reaching out to the next generation.

Back in class, my students commented about how talented and nice so many of the men in prison were. Much as I had come to realize with Tom, they quickly concluded that either the men deserved an Oscar for acting or something had gone terribly wrong in their lives. I discovered that talking about the cobwebs and spiders of these prisoners helped the kids in my class deal with the problems that plagued them in their own lives. The cobwebs were fairly easy to spot: fighting, drug use, school suspensions, multiple sexual relationships or failing grades were pretty common. However, the spiders *creating* these cobwebs were as varied as the kids themselves. For many of the students, the spider was a broken family or the pain they felt because someone they knew and loved had been murdered. Other students realized that their spider was the sense of loss they felt having been abandoned by a parent. Others identified poverty, racial discrimination, low self-esteem or pride. A few students came to me privately and revealed that their spider was the shame and guilt they felt at having been victims of sexual abuse.

Today, 13 years after working with Tom, I have learned a great deal about cobwebs and spiders, both from my life and from the lives of the hundreds of young adults I've worked with through the years. Tom and I both had deep-seated anger issues. But anger was not Tom's spider, nor was it mine. Anger, like overeating, lying, gang-banging and drug-abuse, is a *cobweb*–a sign that the foundation in a particular area of your life is absent or compromised. But like physical pain, anger has a positive quality in that *it lets us know* something on the inside is not right.

Identifying and removing spiders is a life-long process. Understanding that there will always be spiders in your life should provide comfort to those frustrated with the re-emergence of spiders you thought you had diligently removed. One of the most valuable lessons I learned came from the father of the boy Tom murdered. He came to speak at an assembly I organized for the students at my school, and he shared with us the internal work he had done soon after his son was killed to prevent the spiders of hate and revenge from taking hold of his heart. His solution: forgiveness! This response was *unthinkable* for many of us, but this man had realized that he, not Tom, would be the one who suffered if he allowed those spiders to take hold. And if he ever has to deal with these spiders again at some points again his life, he will do so firmly and with courage.

Looking back, I'm convinced that if I had understood and dealt sooner with my low self-esteem and my need to be accepted, I would have been able to avoid many difficult situations, including my assault on the two beautiful girls on the bus. As a counselor, I've come to realize that some of the most violent and angry people in the world are people who have been deeply hurt, but have never dealt with their pain. The reality is that if you struggle with anger, you have only two options: you can control your anger by healing it, or it can control you. There is no middle ground. But understand this: if you allow yourself to become a man controlled by anger, you will live your life being vulnerable to every outside influence, every annoyance—no matter how minor, and every slight—real or imagined. In the end, you will be as much a prisoner as Tom.

Stop fighting cobwebs. Kill the spider.

Adam Cristman

Adam Cristman

Photo credit: Scott Pribyl

Adam Cristman is a professional soccer player and a starting forward for the Kansas City Wizards. Prior to joining the Wizards in 2009, Adam spent two seasons as a starting forward for the New England Revolution. Drafted late in the fourth round, Adam took the professional soccer world by storm his first year, finishing second in Major League Soccer rookie goal-scoring and assists. A member of the Revolution's 18-man senior player squad, he was one of three finalists for the 2007 Gatorade Rookie of the Year. He was named MLS Player of the Week for Week 15 of the 2008 season.

Prior to entering the pros, Adam played for soccer powerhouse University of Virginia (UVA) where he was a four-year starter. While there, he was an ACC All-Freshman, a two-time NSCAA All-South Atlantic Team and an All-ACC Team honoree. As a sophomore, he earned ACC All-Tournament honors when UVA won its ninth ACC conference title. On October 20, 2006, Adam registered UVA soccer's first three-goal hat-trick in 142 games earning him recognition as the ACC Player of the Week, Soccer America Player of the Week, and *College Soccer News* National Player of the Week. That same year, he helped lead UVA to its first NCAA College Cup appearance in nearly a decade.

Adam was a member of both the U-17 and U-18 men's national teams. He was a member of the U.S. U-23 Team for four consecutive years, earning two international caps during the team's tour of Japan in February 2007. He was also in the mix for the 2008 Olympic roster.

A commanding presence on the field, Adam devotes his free time off the field to youth and children's charities.

Editor's Note

I knew I wanted to include at least one young man in this book. I started asking around for names and received many excellent submissions. There was one name, however, that kept coming up time and again: Adam Cristman. This is undoubtedly due, in part, to the fact that Adam is a bit of a local hero where I live: he was a high school soccer star who went on to play for the University of Virginia, the New England Revolution and now the Kansas City Wizards. But ultimately I chose him because his athletic accomplishments, as impressive as they are, pale in comparison to who he is as a person.

Adam was raised in Richmond, Virginia; so, I couldn't help but ask what he thought of those long, cold New England winters. "I'll tell you what," he laughed, "it certainly provided my wife and me with the motivation we need to follow our dream of opening a children's soccer camp in Costa Rica." I thought he was kidding; but, it turns out this is something that Adam and several of his friends have had in the works for years. "It's about doing what I can to provide a saner life for me and my family, while at the same time, hopefully doing something that is of service to others who have less than we do. Plus the surfing is great there!"

I'm delighted to introduce one of the most remarkable young men I've had the pleasure to know, Mr. Adam Cristman.

A Conversation with Adam Cristman

KHJ: *First off, congratulations on an amazing year!*

Adam: Thanks! Thanks very much.

KHJ: *I have to say–I love the fact that you were drafted late, passed over by several teams, and then came out and just blew everyone away. Vindication–I love it!*

Adam: Definitely! It's a good feeling. Part of my motivation this year certainly came from wanting to make the coaches who didn't pick me earlier feel a little regret. (laughs) But yeah, it was a really great year for me. Of course, now that means I'm not the underdog anymore! This season I'm coming in trying to live up to what I did last year.

KHJ: *That's the price of greatness, maybe.*

Adam: Yeah, right. (laughs)

KHJ: *Before we get into the substance of this interview, on behalf of all the aspiring soccer players out there, tell me what it's like playing professional soccer. What is the best part about it?*

Adam: First and foremost is the fact that we're all sort of living a dream. You grow up playing the game and you hope that maybe someday you'll have the opportunity to play at this level; so when that opportunity comes along, it's a pretty incredible feeling. Second, you're getting paid for playing soccer! Plus, personally, I have great guys on my team. So, I just feel like I'm in a really great position right now.

KHJ: *Any down side?*

Adam: I hate to call it a down side because I feel so lucky to be in this position and I don't want to be perceived in any way as complaining. But sure, there are things that challenge me. I think it was Tiki Barber who said that while people saw him on the field, and saw him playing, they didn't see everything it took to get there each week. They never saw him when he was sitting in ice water to alleviate pain in his muscles, or when he was unable to move much the morning after a game because he got hit 30 times in two hours. So there is that element. There is a physical toll on your body, but because it's a job, you have to be mentally willing to push yourself all the time, regardless of how you feel. So, even when it's really, really cold or really, really hot, you get out and you practice or you play. The cold, the heat, the wet–it's all part of the game and sometimes when its 23 degrees, the last thing you want to do is to go outside for three hours. But you have to be there and you have to give it *everything* you've got, *every* single time.

KHJ: *Is that different from before?*

Adam: It is because, as a professional player, you're always fighting for your position. In college, you fought for that starting position also, mostly because you wanted to play. Now, there is the same love of the game; but there is this added layer. I'm fighting for that starting slot because I want to play, but also because my job is at stake. So it becomes a bit of a different beast, I think.

KHJ: *It sounds like you've got to learn to deal with some new elements, though in a familiar environment.*

Adam: Yeah, exactly. But it's part of being an adult–or becoming an adult. And you try to deal with all these new things as best as you can and not let them take you off in one direction or another.

I want to say too that, aside from the actual playing, one other thing I really enjoy about playing at this level is the chance to go into middle schools and high schools, or into soccer camps, and work with kids. Every week there's a different group from our team that goes out into the community–and we sign autographs and take pictures, of course–but we also talk with young players and coach them.

KHJ: *I assume you work mainly with high-level players–travel teams and such.*

Adam: No, not at all. I wouldn't even want that. In fact, just recently I went to a regular high school soccer practice and helped coach for half the practice and then I played in a game with them for the second half. It was great, and I think they had a really good time, you know, seeing what it was like to play against someone at this level.

At the camps especially, we work with players at every level, from recreation league to travel and club leagues. I enjoy it all–across the board. I'm not there just for the star players. What's the fun in that, right? The reality is that not everyone can be great at soccer. But, I believe that with the right encouragement, everyone can be a little bit better. So, when I see a player struggling–you know, maybe one player who just isn't keeping up and he's getting heat from the other players or whatever–I always try to reach out to that kid–take him aside and talk to him. Typically, he is trying to do things too fast–trying to get the ball off too fast. So, I'll tell him, "Hey, slow down. Take an extra touch, control it, and then make a simple pass." I'll get him to do that over and over and, hopefully, by the end of the session he– or she, by the way– is doing it better.

KHJ: *Having worked with different groups and played at all these different levels, I wonder what you see as some of the common denominators among players across the board. In other words, are there things you see that players at every level need in order to be successful?*

Adam: Good question. I'd say it's the fact that everyone needs encouragement when they are trying to learn. You always hear about it when you screw up. Teammates and coaches are going to get frustrated when you make bad plays–that's just the way it is. But if all someone hears is negatives, they aren't going to be as likely to improve–that's my opinion. So if you're on a team, you've got to tell your teammates when they're doing something right–or even when they're starting to do something right. Give each other a reason to keep working at getting better.

I'm playing at a higher level now, but I'm still new to being a professional. So I'm sort of in the same boat as a lot of these kids I work with, and there are days when I feel like I'm the kid who's messing up and I'm looking for someone who'll say to me, "Just take your time. You're fine. You'll get there." That's the truth. I still need some of that positive encouragement. And because I know *I* need it, I've been able to be a little bit better around some of the rookies coming in this year. So when I see one of them having a bad day or if someone seems nervous, I'll try to take a minute to remind him that he can be a success here. He made it here for a reason and he just needs to take a breath, relax and come at it again; and he'll get there.

KHJ: *Switching gears a bit here. You're a good-looking guy, a professional soccer player, traveling all over the world—there is a lot of fun to be had out there for you. Yet here you are, 23 years old and already you've taken the big step into marriage. Most guys your age would think you're crazy!*

Adam: I know, I know. (laughs) But I got very lucky when I met my wife. Ashley and I met when we were 14, started dating when we were 16, and knew when we were 18 that we wanted to get married. Then it was just a matter of waiting for the proper time—four years later, after we'd graduated from college—to finally take our vows.

KHJ: *With that in mind, I'm really interested in getting your take on something. I admit I am old and very likely out of touch, however (yes, the big "however!") I can't help but notice the one-dimensional way in which women are portrayed in media, especially media aimed at young men. I'm thinking specifically of the hyped-up sexual image that is so pervasive. Of course, I'm not naïve enough to think that anything we can say will stop guys from watching sexy videos or flipping through magazines or whatever.*

Adam: No. But I think it's reasonable to suggest to young guys that they might want to think about the images coming across the screen. Maybe try to define yourself and your sense of right and wrong a little more clearly before you find yourself watching that stuff without a second thought. Every single one of those girls is somebody's daughter or sister. They're human beings and, just based on that, they deserve at least a passing thought from *whoever* is watching them. I think it's fair to ask guys to maybe take a second to ask yourself how you would feel if this was your sister, or a girl you knew or a girl you *cared about*. Is this what you would want? Is it something you'd be okay with for her?

KHJ: *Is that a tall order, asking young men to do that?*

Adam: Maybe. But we just seem so willing to take in all this garbage and never really question it. "Sex sells," so goes the cliché. And the media isn't going to stop. As long as they get people to watch they're going to keep putting it out there. They don't care about whether it's respectful or hurtful, or even right or wrong. So it's up to us, as consumers, to be smart and to care a bit more about these women and how they're portrayed in the movies and videos and all the rest of the stuff we "love" so much.

KHJ: *And the bottom line is that it's not reality, this sexed-up view of women. It's not how women are and it's not how real relationships are.*

Adam: Exactly. It's like saying, "If you went to see *Jurassic Park*, would you believe that there are really dinosaurs roaming around somewhere in Hawaii?" It's fake. It's a fake image created by Hollywood.

KHJ: *You're married to a very pretty girl. But obviously you don't relate to her only on that level.*

Adam: No. But when I started dating Ashley, like I said, that was it. I knew very quickly that she was the one. And from that point forward, my goal changed from the more typical goals guys have toward women—which maybe aren't great to the goal of being the kind of man she could be proud of. I wanted to be the kind of guy that her friends would look at and say, "She is so lucky!" And not because I was some big soccer player or because of the way I looked—*nothing* like that. I wanted to be someone in her life who treated her so well and with so much respect that she never had to doubt me or herself or us. That was how I wanted, and want, to be measured. Am I thoughtful of her? Am I kind? I mean, I definitely want to be the best at my job—which right now is soccer—and every day I go out and try to be the number one guy on the field; and when I'm not, it definitely brings me down, you know—it really bums me out. But, how well I can play soccer isn't how I measure myself as a man, or as a person.

KHJ: *Looking in as an outsider, I would think that it would be hard for young guys to really believe that they can or should measure themselves by that standard. That's not what they're told. They're told to go after the women and the power and the money. That is how the culture pushes boys to define themselves.*

Adam: True. But, you know and this reminds me of something I was thinking about a couple of days ago—when you talk to little boys, they all want to grow up to be policemen, firemen and superheroes. My friends and I used to play cops all the time when I was nine or ten. Even when I was a little older, say 11 or 12 or so, I had a group of kids in my neighborhood join me in a Navy Seals club doing missions, fitness tests, et cetera.

You fast-forward a few more years, and most kids will tell you they want to be rock stars, athletes, movie stars or just plain rich—more selfish dreams, for sure. But still, that first instinct is to want to grow up to be someone who helps others, someone who serves the greater good. Where does all that go?

I look around now and what I see is this enormous emphasis on movie stars and athletes. I agree that movies can inspire and entertain us and that great athletes can bring cities and people together by giving them something to support. But their "deeds" are pretty superficial, very temporary and largely forgotten. The sports star is a "hero" until the next game comes around; the big celebrity until the next film opens. And the real tragedy in this is that the true heroes—like the men and women fighting in Iraq and Afghanistan or the men and women in the Coast Guard who saved many lives in the Katrina effort—are virtually overlooked. We should learn *their* names and remember how lucky we are to have them around.

Instead, we are force-fed an unrealistic image of what a hero is. We are sold on this lifestyle that is [the purview of] a select few—mainly movie stars, rock stars and rappers living the "Hollywood" dream. It leaves a lot of people feeling more fickle than ever: complaining about high gas prices and the inability to drive the Hummer or to buy the mansion with the infinity pool that we see on MTV.

Maybe this is more ranting than assessing and providing answers for building a better future; but in general, I think that the changes I've seen on TV, in the movies, et cetera—even in the few years since I was a teenager—require some serious reassessment. We are trading character, moral fiber and respect for material wealth, poor decision-making and lives without substance. That's a bad deal any way you look at it.

KHJ: *I agree. I just find all the fascination with TV, videos, et cetera, to be sort of ironic in this sense: most young men and women are pretty quick to question authority, or what they perceive as authority. But in my opinion, the true authority in a person's life is the one he or she fails to question. Looking at it this way, parents and teachers are not the true authorities in a young person's life. (I have kids and believe me, they have no problem questioning what I tell them!) But anything Hollywood, anything film- or video- or music-related they take in without a whole lot of thought.*

Moving on! What quality do you most admire in people?

Adam: I really admire people who don't put on a *persona* that is different around one group versus another. So, they're not around the popular kids doing one thing and then around the Christian kids and acting like a saint. It's being true to yourself–defining yourself and then staying true to that; that I think is the most admirable thing you can do as a person. Tony Dungy* is probably the best living example of this, in my opinion. When you look at what he's been through and then at the way he has stayed true to everything he believes in, it is such an inspiration.

I think this quality is true of a lot of good men. They have figured out who they are and then they are true to that. They don't change because of circumstance or because it might make it easier.

Unfortunately, athletics are as much about image these days as they are about ability. Even now I still see guys struggling to be true to who they really are. I'll give you an example. There is this one guy, a big starter [in the MLS]. When he's out in front of people he's always doing wild stuff; he's the "class clown" kind of guy–always making jokes, always loud. But when you get him alone, he's a really solid guy. And I just wish he was like that all the time. I wish that's what kids who watch him would see. But I think he feels like he needs to be Mr. Cool out there. And I think, again, this is where the media comes in. All the attention is so focused on these "high profile" people–like they're the only ones who matter. Or like the only way to be someone is to be popular, act cool and all that, even if that's not who you really are. And, you know, that's just ridiculous.

KHJ: *You sound exhausted just talking about it.*

Adam: I just don't know the answer and that's frustrating. You can look back even one generation and see that families used to be the focus–the hub of life. Now families are really spread out and so their influence is less than say, the media, which is everywhere. In place of family values passed on naturally, the media has given us more and more emphasis on sleeping around, random hookups and drunken encounters as the normal way of life.

My wife's family gets together every year during the week between

---

*Tony Dungy was the long-time head coach of the Indianapolis Colts.

Christmas and New Year's. We cram 23 people into a one-story rancher that has three bedrooms and one and a half baths. Whenever I tell people that, they say, "Oh my gosh, that sounds miserable! You don't get any space or any privacy." But it's awesome. It is one of the greatest weeks of the year. There are so many people around and you get to have these great, open and honest conversations. One minute I'm playing with a seven-year-old; the next I'll be talking sports with her uncles or spending time with her grandparents.

In the so-called "real world," the focus always seems to be on "How much can I get?" and "How do I get more?" Like this is how we become men! But when I think about the best men I know, it has nothing to do with how much they have materially. It is all about who they are, the kindness they show to their family, how much their kids love them. These are the guys you want to grow up to be like. The fact that Ashley's grandfather and father have raised families who love to come together for a week in this tiny house just to be together–*those* are great men.

KHJ: *Are you willing to do a little word association?*

Adam: Sure.

KHJ: *Bullies.*

Adam: Empty. Wanting.

KHJ: *Compassion.*

Adam: Friendship.

KHJ: *Boys don't cry.*

Adam: Baloney, everybody cries. If we don't, we're just hiding from something.

KHJ: *Respect for women.*

Adam: It's key. Like we said earlier, the lack of respect is huge–a huge problem.

Dee Bradley Baker

Dee Bradley Baker

Photo credit: Baker family

You may not know Dee Baker's name, but if you watch TV, go to the movies, or play video games, then you've heard his voice—a lot. He is the "go-to guy" in Hollywood for creating realistic animal, alien or monster sounds and is considered one of the most versatile and sought-after voice actors working in the entertainment industry today. Dee's credits include the voice of Daffy Duck and the Tasmanian Devil, along with scores of characters and creatures he brings to life on film, television, and in video games. You can hear him daily on TV in everything from Nickelodeon's *SpongeBob SquarePants* to Fox television's *American Dad!* and Cartoon Network's *Cow and Chicken*. He recently wrapped up work on George Lucas' animated *Star Wars* series.

His long list of interactive video game credits includes "Halo 2 & 3," "Lord of the Rings: The Hobbit" and "X-Men Legends 1 and 2." His even longer list of movie credits includes *Pirates of the Caribbean, Dawn of the Dead, Happy Feet,* and *Space Jam.*

Editor's Note

I have no earthly idea how Dee Baker is able to do what he does. I mean, the Daffy Duck voice, maybe I can understand that. I can sort of even get my head around some of the strange, alien sounds he makes. But listening to, oh, let's say, his cricket noises, makes my head spin. Because Dee doesn't make cricket-ish noises. No sir. Dee makes sounds that are exactly like a cricket's. His chirps and trills are indistinguishable from the real thing. It's like having a biblical plague in your living room. And don't even get me started on the frogs. Or the ducks. Or the cats. Oh, forget it. Just go and listen for yourself at www.deebaker.com.

In the meantime, it's my pleasure to introduce the insanely talented Mr. Dee Baker.

Fail!

Here is my advice to you: fail.

Seek out and embrace failure every day. For without failure you are sunk.

If anyone asks you what you learned from the essay by that voice-over guy who makes weird voices and sounds for cartoons and video games, go ahead and tell them, "Oh, he advised me to fail."

I know this sounds ridiculous, but I really do have a point. I see failure as an essential and often maligned life tool. And it turns out, a big part of being an actor is constant failure. Forget talent and persistence; that's assumed. The number one job qualification for being an actor is tolerating, and even enjoying, relentless failure—having doors slammed in your face every day. Smart actors feed on it and use it to their advantage. Even after an actor reaches what seems like "success," the ability to court failure through calculated risk, sometimes risking spectacular failure, can be a good sign of a vital creative spirit and successful career.

I first became friends with failure doing plays and musicals as a kid. I found that live audiences are great at letting you know immediately when you are failing. Later, I found an even better arena for failure—stand up comedy, where the honest, real-time feedback of an audience is much more prevalent than with plays. There I learned that honest failure can be the best of teachers. You instantly know when a joke works, but more importantly, you know when a joke fails. And if you honestly acknowledge failure, the audience will be on your side and they will laugh *with* you. Try to cover up failure and they laugh *at* you.

I found that this is a principle that can be more broadly applied: no matter what the endeavor, no matter what your level of achievement, honest mistakes and real-time feedback (even if painful) are pure gold. Failure is pure gold. Without it you will get nowhere. I say to you: strive to fail honestly and openly a lot.

Now don't get me wrong. I'm not encouraging failure for its own sake or celebrating incompetence or self-destruction. No, no, no. My point is you should strive to fail *meaningfully*, recognize it, heed its insights and then use failure to your advantage. Otherwise, you are like my computer, which is great at failing at all kinds of things, over and over without variation. (I want to throw it out the window right now, but I've got to finish this essay.) A computer never changes course, never uses its failure as a learning tool, never tinkers with its failure strategy. We humans, however, usually either just give up, or if we are bullheaded, we just keep repeating the same mistakes over and over again like my laptop.

If you want to study with a master of effective failing, check out a baby. They are black belts at failing effectively. Ever seen a baby trying to walk? They fall down again and again and again. All day long, day after day, a pre-toddling infant will resolutely and creatively fail to walk with an endless variety of spectacular wipeouts. Babies are way smarter than grownups. In fact, babies are Perfect Learning Machines because they use their trips, face-plants, and crashes to modify their tactics when learning to walk. Physically and mentally, babies learn more rapidly and with greater leaps than you or I ever will. They are hard-wired, so to speak, to experiment with failure. They don't take failure so personally. That's why one day little button-eyed Brittney-Brianna crawls and stumbles and the next day she walks through a doorway. You've witnessed a miraculous, quantum leap. All thanks to masterful failing.

Typically, the older we get, the less failure we seek or allow ourselves. We try to do everything "right." We build failure out of our lives, sending it away rather than welcoming its insights. We think if we fail, we lose. As a result, we stop learning, we stop growing, we stop living.

So, how can you use effective failing to find a fun career and generally improve your life? Here are some ideas:

1. Fearlessly find what you love to do by failing at lots of things you think you might like.

Don't limit your life by pursuing only things you are really good at (that you can't fail at). Try stuff you might like regardless of your ability. Let yourself experimentally "fail" at what is fun for you. I went to a great little liberal arts college where I studied biology, fine arts, the German language and philosophy because I thought they were fun. Turns out I wasn't particularly great at any of them nor passionate enough about any to pursue them professionally. (I spent very little time thinking about a "career" at all until I was in my early 30s, in fact.) During college I did a lot of live performing on the side, which I was very good at. I took only one acting class. I focused my study time on what I liked but wasn't great at, while continuing to practice and gain experience and confidence in what I loved and was *very* good at.

Luckily, my parents and teachers encouraged me to cultivate the habit of doing things I loved to do, regardless of how much I failed at any of them and regardless of any prospects of future monetary payoff. This habit has paid off many times throughout my life, and has led me in my own crooked way to a splendidly fun career. Cultivate the life habit of doing things you love. It will always pay off and it's the best way I know of to find yourself.

2. Fearlessly find what you're good at.

This is initially a separate project from finding things you love. Everyone has at least a few of these they can be very good at. Smart use of failure can help you find a few options here.

3. Blind Failure Type #1: Just because you are good at something doesn't mean you should make a career out of it.

Many people are miserable prisoners of something they are very good at. They are incredibly good at something that fails to make them happy, fails to stimulate, fails to deliver any fun, fails to improve. There is no sign of failure on the outside, yet inside there is a failure overload that they ignore. And failure is no good if you don't listen to it. Find things you're good at. But be aware of your internal sense of failure—misery, boredom, et cetera. If it continues to build, without changing, leveling off or decreasing, this could mean it's not right for you. You may be brilliant at it, impress parents and friends, even earn a lot of money doing it, but earning a living doing something you hate is toxic. Don't be blind to your inner sense of failure. Some things are just not right for you no matter how good you are at them.

4. Blind Failure Type #2: Just because you love doing something doesn't mean you should make a career of it, either.

On the flip side, blindly pursuing something that everyone else agrees you actually suck at for career purposes is also a big mistake. Here, instead of not listening to your own feedback, you ignore or avoid the feedback of others. If you stop listening to good, steady, accurate external failure data, it is impossible to gain an honest take on your ability, take corrective action or improve. This is essentially a self-deluded hobbyist –people who think they are great but they really aren't. Worst of all, they don't really want to know this. Many sad people maintain this kind of delusion. You may love doing it, but you must inform your love with good, honest objective input if you want to follow this into a career. There's no shame in having a hobby. Accept it, continue to have fun with it, but move on to something else when you want to earn a living.

5. Target the intersection of what you love with what you're really good at, for there lies your career.

That, in a nutshell, is the best advice I can give you in finding a career. People who have found that are the ones who say, "I've got the best job in the world." Don't you want to be that person? Betcha do. Failure can help point the way. This intersection is where you will find the "well-placed confidence" that will satisfy you and that people will hire. People don't hire mere skill or talent–they hire well-placed confidence.

6. Never stop failing at what you love and are good at.

Just because you're good at something you love doesn't mean you can't or shouldn't fail at it. You can always get better, learn more, increase your confidence in doing what you love. And you can't do that without continued experimental failure. Stop failing and you will eventually get as bored as a four-year-old at an opera. No matter how good you are, doing the same old thing gets boring without fresh variation, risk taking, and missteps. Keep finding new ways to fail and learn from that and you'll always grow as you expand your grasp of the thing you love doing so well.

7. How can you start failing today?

You will be living the dream as long as you are willing to follow what you love, take chances, and happily fail. Have fun becoming who you are. Ever seen a baby laugh after wiping out? That's the way to do it.

Just never forget to fail.

Dominique Wilkins

Dominique Wilkins

Photo credit: Atlanta Hawks

NBA Hall of Famer and basketball legend Dominique Wilkins, aka the "Human Highlight Film," burst onto the NBA scene in 1982 as a first-round draft pick (third overall) out of the University of Georgia. Following a stellar rookie season, he was named to the NBA's All-Rookie Team in 1983. In his second year, he averaged 21.6 points per game, beginning a scoring streak that would see him average at least 20 points per game over the next 11 seasons, including a career high of 30.3 points per game in 1986 (a feat that garnered him the NBA scoring title that year). In 1988, he scored an incredible 29 points in 30 minutes of playing time. Four years later, he would again pull out all the stops sinking 23 free throws in one game without a miss.

This two-time winner of the NBA Slam-Dunk Championship was named to seven All-NBA teams and nine All-Star squads. He is one of only 12 players in NBA history to score over 25,000 points, is ranked ninth on the all-time scoring list with 26,668 points and eleventh in career scoring average at 24.8 points per game.

Dominique retired from professional basketball in 1999. The Hawks retired his jersey (#21) in 2001–only the third player in the franchise's history to be so honored. He was inducted into the NBA Hall of Fame in 2006.

Dominique Wilkins is currently the Atlanta Spirit's vice president of basketball.

Editor's Note

I have only limited memories of my meeting with Dominique Wilkins. Okay–that's not true. But what is true is that my recollection is clouded by the drama that led up to it. I had been given 30 minutes with him–a generous offer considering he had squeezed me into his schedule before he had to leave for court to finalize the adoption of his child. As I drove through downtown Atlanta on my way to his office, I was unexpectedly rerouted through a construction detour–a move that proved to be my downfall. I arrived at his office sweaty, out-of-breath and, worst of all, 10 minutes late.

I would have understood had he been upset with me when I finally stumbled into his office. Instead, he calmly offered me a moment to get my bearings and waited patiently as I got my notes together. "We'll get this thing done," he reassured me as we finally sat down to talk. And so we did.

What I learned, both in this interview and in a subsequent meeting, is that Dominique Wilkins is a class act. He is confident without being egotistical, compassionate without being soft. To look at him today, it is hard to imagine he was once the kid who was bullied at school, and told time and again that he would never make it in the NBA. Dominique is a real-life example of someone who found a way to reach deep within himself and rise above both the bullies and the naysayers to become a superstar. He is a self-made man in the best and truest sense of the word.

Though he hardly needs an introduction, it is my pleasure to introduce the "Human Highlight Film," Mr. Dominique Wilkins.

A Conversation with Dominique Wilkins

KHJ: When we look at the world around us, we can see the places where we get it right in today's culture and places where we get it wrong.

Dominique: The thing I see as one of the biggest misconceptions out there—and I see it across the spectrum—is this idea that disrespect is respect. A lot of young men and a lot of male role models in music, movies and television behave in a way that is disrespectful to women, to each other and to the world in general. It's all about being as tough as you can be and as "big" as you can be—a big focus on self. But I think they've got it backwards. The truth is you build respect through the courage and kindness that you show others, not by trying to show how tough you are, how much money you have and all that. That's not respect. You can't *buy* respect. Maybe you can buy a form of respect—envy, really—for a little while. But eventually when all the money and attention are gone, what do you have?

KHJ: I agree. But everywhere we look, we see young, cocky millionaires who behave this way and do so with almost total impunity. And, I think, most young men look at these guys and think, "That's what I want." And it's hard for them to get away from that kind of thinking.

Dominique: Absolutely. And I understand it's not easy out there today for young men. I've said many times that the *easiest* thing for a person to do is to be an entertainer or an athlete or something of that nature. The hardest thing is to become is a young woman or a young man of genuine character. But you've got to do it! You have got to build your own character, and you can't use someone else—especially negative influences out there—to do that. It won't work.

KHJ: There is a big controversy right now over how the younger generation of men—and women to a lesser degree—carry themselves, specifically what they wear and how they talk.

Dominique: I grew up believing that when you looked good, you played good, and when you played good, you projected a positive image to the public. So, my son knows he can't come into my house with his pants hanging off of him. He can't come with the big baggy t-shirts and talking slang—not in my house, because I know that the things he does now and the choices he makes now will affect what he does and who he becomes in the future. If you want to have a successful and fulfilling life, you start by making smart choices about things like how you dress and how you carry yourself. And you surround yourself with the right people, especially in school. A lot of people, a lot of so-called role models, don't know the right or wrong thing to do. It depends on the atmosphere that they grew up in and who they had around when they were young. So you've got to be smart. Don't just follow some actor or rapper or athlete because he's famous! Educate yourself to the point where you can make good, smart choices and surround yourself with the right people.

KHJ: *When you talk about education, it sounds as though you're talking about a lot more than just formal classroom learning.*

Dominique: Oh, absolutely. You know, I do a lot of speaking around the country on diabetes and hypertension, and the message that I try to get out there is that education and knowledge are key to your future. For example, a lot of people don't know that they're diabetic or that they have hypertension, and they don't know what the long-term effects from these chronic diseases are because they don't have the education. So it's up to people like me working with these big companies to get the word out there. The same thing applies to everyday life. For example, in athletics—since I know more about that—there's a short window where you make a ton of money. But generally, it's a very short career. Then you have the rest of your life to live. What do you do when all the fame and fortune are gone? What do you have left? The only thing you have left is your self-respect and the relationships you've built.

KHJ: *Well, you have a pile of money. And there is a feeling out there that money can, at some level, make you happier.*

Dominique: No, no way. I mean, being poor definitely isn't easy. But I've been on both ends of the money stick and I can tell you for a fact that you can have all the money in the world and be totally miserable—maybe you're with someone you're not happy with or maybe you're in an environment you're not happy with. I know many people who have a lot of money who are very, very stressed out. So money doesn't buy happiness. It can maybe put a nice down-payment on it. But it's a short-term down-payment. If you look to money to solve all your problems, it's a very, very short road you're going down. Sure you'll feel good for awhile. You'll feel pleasure. But from a "real-life" standpoint, you've got to be able to lose everything and still cope.

I grew up poor with eight brothers and sisters and one parent. So I know what it's like to live that way. I know how hard it is. But that is why you must constantly educate yourself and constantly try to live the best way you can. From a business and life standpoint, this is what is *required*. Basketball is my first love, but I do a lot of things outside of athletics, and I have been successful at them because I've taken the time to learn and I've been smart enough to surround myself with people who can help me grow and help me stay in the right frame of mind. It's again—and I can't stress it enough—it's about making sure you educate yourself because the more education you have, the more successful you will be. Knowledge *is* key.

KHJ: *Let's talk for a minute about young men in middle school and high school. You have six kids, so you have a good feel for what life is like for a lot of young men. I'd like to talk about having the courage to stand up for yourself or for someone else or for what you believe in.*

Dominique: I think what is especially difficult is for a young man to take a step back and *question* what is going on around him. But you have to question what you see around you, especially with your peers—especially with your peers! Because your peers can be very persuasive and you know, as a young man, when you feel like you don't fit in with your peers, you feel like you're doing something wrong. But the truth is that you don't have to be with the in-crowd to be respected. I've never been that kind of person. In fact, when I was young I was probably the odd kid out because everybody thought I was this quiet, shy kid and everybody else was outgoing. The guys who were popular were the ones who loved to get in trouble—most kids figured that was cool. But that wasn't cool to me. It's not cool to do what somebody else is doing just because it sounds good or just because it's somehow expected of you by your peers, especially if you know it's wrong. You've got to make your own decisions in life; you make your own way.

KHJ: *But the end result of that, of course, is that you may be perceived as being different. You risk being singled out.*

Dominique: That's true, but so what? You don't have to be like everybody else. It's *okay* to be a little different. There's nothing wrong with being different. Because at the end of the day, when you're doing things you know are right, and you take that long road instead of that short road to success, at the end, you're going to be looking at these people and saying, "You know what, these are the things I tried to tell you a long time ago." You have to have long-term goals and a long-term focus to be successful. I had to learn that lesson very early in life because I've been on my own since I was 16. So, whether I wanted to or not, I had to sort of educate myself, through school, through the streets, and right on into athletics. It's something that I'm very proud of.

KHJ: *In the speech you gave when you were inducted into the Hall of Fame, you talked about your nephew Damien and the fact that, at the start of his career, nobody believed in him or his ability to play. I want to quote you. You said, "He's been through a lot. Nobody believed this kid could play. [But] I remember telling him, 'Hey, there's nothing wrong with making it the hard way.' . . . [H]e proved all the doubters wrong, and now he's an NBA player with the Seattle SuperSonics."*

Dominique: I said that because I wanted him to know how proud I was of him and because I know what it's like to have people doubt you. I came up through my life with people telling me what I couldn't do, that I wouldn't be successful or I wouldn't amount to anything. My whole life!

KHJ: *Who told you that?*

Dominique: Everyone! I heard it from my peers and in some instances my family–not my immediate family–but other family members used to tell me, "You'll never make it into the NBA. You'll never be a player." And I remember vividly saying, "Not only am I going to make it, but I'm going to be one of the best who ever played." And they laughed.

KHJ: *What do you say to young men who might be hearing the same kind of negativity today, whether it is in terms of athletics or intellect or just dreams they have for the future?*

Dominique: I would say to those young men that, when someone hurts you that way, *you hold your head up high. You keep the faith*! You keep your belief in yourself because no one can take that from you no matter what they say. As long as you have that faith in yourself, and you have a goal, no one can touch you with their doubts and negativity. In fact, what you should do is allow that to fuel you to work even harder to prove them wrong. There's nothing like proving people wrong through success! You don't have to say a word. That's what I've done my whole life. Even when I was in the NBA and I'd done well and become one of the best players, many people still didn't want to give me the credit I had earned. So it made me work that much harder. And it took a while to get there, but now I'm at that point where I *am* recognized as one of the best who ever played. My entry into the Hall of Fame finally put the doubts to rest. But, it took me believing in myself, being patient, never getting upset about what someone said or the respect I thought I should have gotten. I just held my tongue and did the things I knew I needed to do to keep my self-respect, because things will come back around. They may not come around when you want, but they will come around.

KHJ: *What's the biggest misconception about what it means to be a man?*

Dominique: Well, when I grew up, a man was a guy who went to school, graduated, got a good job, worked hard, and came home and took care of his family.

KHJ: *That's a pretty good definition of a man.*

Dominique: I think it's a good definition. That's what the hard-working, blue-collar worker was like back in those days. Those are the people who I have more respect for because they put it all on the line every day and every night. Those are my heroes. Athletes are not my heroes. I've got a lot of friends who are athletes, but the guys I admire the most are ordinary people who battle it out every day to support their families. One of the guys I admired most growing up—actually it was a couple of guys. One was my high school coach who provided me with guidance when I was a young man and helped me believe in myself. The others were guys on the street— the winos on the street—who took me aside in that troubled environment and said, "You know what, we see an opportunity for you. We're gonna make sure you learn and that you get your education. You learn this game of basketball and you respect this game so that you can be the first to get out of this neighborhood." And those "street" guys were the ones who really mentored me, kept me out of trouble, made sure I got to school on time, and even made sure I ate. Those guys are the ones who taught me the right way. Don't get me wrong, there aren't a lot of people out there who are like that. A lot of guys who are the same type of people are very self-serving and, because they didn't make it, they don't want to see you make it. But these guys–my guys–weren't like that. These guys cared enough about me that they didn't want to see me doing the wrong things.

KHJ: *Gov. Doug Wilder had a very similar story–that it was the older gentlemen in his community who shined shoes or sat in the barbershop, who pushed him to excel, to get his education and to make something of himself.*

Dominique: Yeah. I remember whenever I used to get in trouble–or they *thought* I was getting into trouble–they used to come around and slap me upside my head. It was like, "If we catch you out here, this is what's going to happen to you every time. And, we're going to make sure your mom knows about it." And I definitely didn't want her to know! So, they straightened me out, they really did. And at my induction into the Hall of Fame, I made sure I recognized those guys from the old neighborhood because they were a big reason why I was there–especially when you come out of a neighborhood that had the highest crime rate in America. That was a big obstacle to overcome.

KHJ: *Growing up in that neighborhood, you understand better than most folks the real dangers of violence. Yet television, music and video games portray violence and toughness as an essential element of masculinity.*

Dominique: Violence is senseless. Period. And when you're dealing with violence, when you embrace it, be it in video games or on the streets, pretty soon you think that it's normal. You think that's the way life is. But life is not that way. A "real" man is not a violent man.

I would say 95-97 percent of all violent people have personal issues in their lives that they can't overcome, and so they try to use other people's weakness and other people's success to satisfy their own faults and misfortunes in life. And it's wrong, because at the end of the day all you do is hurt someone else's family and you hurt yourself. You're also likely to hurt your own family because, if you wind up in jail, now they have someone who is missing from their lives, maybe for a long time. Violence is just senseless! It is fear-based. And our kids see it and they breathe it; they think that it's cool to be that kind of tough guy, but they are wrong. And, unfortunately, sometimes dead wrong.

KHJ: *What's cool to Dominique Wilkins?*

Dominique: What's cool is to get your education and *do* something in life: be a doctor, a nurse, a lawyer–or an athlete or entertainer. But pursue what you want in life and be successful at it so that you can look back at some point in the future and say, "You know what? I can be happy with the way my life turned out because I made a commitment to myself to be somebody, and I did it on my terms." There's no better feeling in the world than feeling successful. That is the *best* feeling in the world. And to know that you did it yourself? That you built it from scratch? Nothing can touch that. Violence is easy. Being man enough to work and to build a life for yourself and your family–that's hard.

KHJ: *There was a young man in my son's high school–not a particularly popular kid–who was being harassed in the lunch room by a group of the more popular guys. It wasn't the kind of overt stuff you could really call them on. They did things like calling him names as they "coughed" or throwing small bits of food his way.*

Dominique: That happened to me.

KHJ: *To you?*

Dominique: To *me*. And the first thing I would tell a kid in that situation is that you have a right to stand up for yourself. Now, let me say upfront that, in most situations, I tell kids to just walk away. You just need to walk away and not indulge in that. But if you have a situation like that one where someone is constantly picking on you, you have to be ready to take a stand in some form or fashion.

Take my situation for example. I told these kids, "You guys can throw whatever you want at me, you can hit me, you can call me bad names, but you can never take away who I am. So if you want to disrespect me, you go and take your best shot but I'm not going to sit down. I'm not going to lie down. You knock me down and I'll get back up twice."

You can't be afraid to stand up for yourself. And, by the way, it doesn't take violence to do that. If you take a firm stance on who you are as a person, people do think about it. They'll notice and they'll think about it.

I can tell you straight up that most bullies are cowards. Most bullies are cowards because they need other people to validate who they are. They need that crowd to praise them and see how cool and tough they are. I had to face a bully in high school and he was the toughest guy around. Everyone was so afraid of this guy because he took their money, made them do his homework, everything. But I challenged him, and the funny thing is that when I did, other people who I didn't really know stood up with me. Now, in this instance, standing up to this bully meant getting physical. Sometimes it has to be that way. I actually got in a fight with this guy and won, and then, of course, I was the favored guy. Again, I don't advocate violence, but there are times when you've got to stand up for yourself that way.

KHJ: *What about when you see someone else being bullied or mistreated?*

Dominique: I know it's hard as hell to do it, but you need to stand up for that kid. You don't have to fight anybody. But you need to be firm and you need to tell those other kids, "You know what, you need to leave this kid alone. He's done nothing to you guys, so quit picking on him." It takes a lot of courage to speak up in that situation, but that's what a man does.

KHJ: *If you were to share only one piece of wisdom that you have learned throughout your life, what would it be?*

Dominique: Be a giving person. There is an old cliché that it is better to give than to receive, and I believe it is true. Throughout my life, I have been a giving person, perhaps to a fault. Looking back, I'd say that that was my best quality–I gave to others as hard as I received. And what I mean by giving is not just donating money, which is important, but showing respect and kindness to others, taking time with people to try and understand their problems and seeing if you can help. One of the most rewarding things in life is seeing a smile on somebody else's face and knowing you helped put it there. I believe that this is what men do. And we can do it through charity or in passing on some type of wisdom to someone else or by being willing to lend a hand when it is needed. I try to practice this in my own home, where I help my wife with things like cooking and cleaning. When people ask me why I do that, why I don't leave it to my wife, I tell them that I do it because that's what partners do: it's what men do. Marriage–a cohesive marriage–is a 50/50 deal.

KHJ: *If you had the chance to go back and talk to your 15-year-old self, what would you tell him?*

Dominique: You know what I would do? I would teach him all the things I had to learn on my own when I was a kid. I never had that consistent guidance in my life that comes from a father or an uncle or another close male figure, so I was left to learn about life and how to build a life on my own. I did it, but I did it alone. So, if I could go back and talk to my 15-year-old self, I would take the time to show that kid how to make good choices. I'd build a format for him to follow and hope that he'd be diligent enough to follow it. Every kid, every person, deserves that much.

I try to offer the same thing to young men and women when I talk to them. I consider this part of my responsibility as a role model and as a successful man. When you attain success, you give back. You extend a hand to the next guy and to the next generation.

The Honorable L. Douglas Wilder

The Honorable L. Douglas Wilder

Photo credit: Christopher P. Dettmar

The Honorable L. Douglas ("Doug") Wilder holds a unique and extraordinary position in American history as both the grandson of slaves and the first African American in the history of the United States to be elected governor of a state.

An attorney by trade, Doug Wilder graduated from Howard University Law School in 1959. After several years in private practice, he entered the world of politics, rising through the ranks as state senator, lieutenant governor and finally, the governor of Virginia. Under his administration, Virginia was voted the best-managed state in the country by *World Financial* magazine for two consecutive years.

He has been the driving force behind several historic campaigns, including the creation of both the National Slavery Museum in Fredericksburg, Virginia, and the creation of a state holiday to honor civil rights leader Dr. Martin Luther King, Jr. In 1996 Norfolk State University honored him with its creation of the L. Douglas Wilder Performing Arts Center. Virginia Commonwealth University followed suit in 2004 when it renamed its School of Government and Public Affairs the L. Douglas Wilder School of Government and Public Affairs, where he currently serves as a distinguished professor.

He is the recipient of more than three dozen honorary degrees and countless awards, including the NAACP Spingarn Medal, the Anna Eleanor Roosevelt Medallion of Honor, and the Thurgood Marshall Award of Excellence. In his early years, he served in the Korean War and was awarded the Bronze Star Medal for his valor in rescuing wounded GIs and capturing enemy soldiers.

In May of 2004, troubled by the declining conditions in his hometown of Richmond, Doug Wilder threw his hat into the ring for mayor. It came as little surprise when this hometown hero won by a landslide, with more than *75 percent* of the vote!

Editor's Note

From all outward appearances, Doug Wilder's start in life was impossibly difficult. The grandson of slaves, he grew up poor and in the segregated South. Yet, his name will be recorded in every history textbook from this generation forward. Why? Because Doug Wilder is the first African-American in the history of our country to be elected governor of a state. Not just any state either, but his home state of Virginia–the former capital of the Confederacy. That he could experience any measure of success in the face of so much injustice and hardship is awe-inspiring. That he would rise above it to become governor of Virginia is nothing short of miraculous. However, as he will tell you, he was raised with certain intangible advantages that made it possible–more than possible even–for him to succeed at whatever he chose to do.

Doug Wilder is a force of nature, as charming a person as he is demanding. His unparalleled success throughout his political and professional career is due in no small part to his "take-no-prisoners" style–a style that has earned him as many admirers as it has critics. He is alternately portrayed as the quintessential southern gentleman or the fierce politician. However, in the time I've spent with him, I have found him to be neither of these extremes.

I met Governor Wilder for the first time the day I went to his office to ask him if he would consider writing an essay for this book. I began my "pitch" by talking about him: his life, his career, and all that he had experienced, overcome and, ultimately, accomplished. He brushed that aside with a smile. He wasn't interested in talking about himself that day. Instead, as he mulled over my request, he began telling me stories about his mother and father and the ways in which they had softened the jagged corners of poverty for him and his siblings so that it never threatened to consume their lives. He reminisced about the older black men in his neighborhood where he grew up who, having had no real opportunity to go to school themselves, instilled in him a profound understanding of the importance of education. They offered themselves up as living examples of opportunity lost and forged in him a deep appreciation for the power of a strong mind.

At one point toward the end of our meeting, he stood up from his desk and walked over to a small stack of papers that were neatly arranged on a stand and brought them over for me to see. They were letters he had received from children across Virginia. He seemed to remember the names and faces of each one whom he had met, and was obviously moved and invigorated by the memories.

"I am part of the older generation now," he says in his essay that follows, "and we are charged with the task of successfully instilling in your generation an understanding and appreciation of the travails that have been overcome and what it takes to overcome them." I like to think that this line came from those final moments of our meeting—when he looked at the letters from the children, reflected for a moment at the innumerable awards and honors that blanketed his wall, and then turned and told me to add his name to my list.

I am honored to introduce Virginia's history-making governor, the Honorable L. Douglas Wilder.

The Mediocrity Trap

One has to resist the temptation to rhapsodize over his life's beginnings. I have often referred to my childhood family status as "gentle" poverty. I use the softening term "gentle" to rid any impression of being impoverished in the general sense. I was the next to the youngest in a close-knit family of 10 children. Sadly, my oldest sister died at age three, and the next eldest, a boy yet unnamed, died near childbirth. There were six girls and two boys, and my best friend was my older brother, Robert, who we all called Bob. Although he was 10 years older than I, he treated me as if I was his regular sidekick and carried me everywhere he went–sometimes being criticized by his peers for "always having *him* tag along."

I also use the softening term "gentle" because the ravages of poverty were absent in our home, despite the fact that my father's parents–my grandparents–were born into slavery! When my grandparents came out of slavery, in order to have a new start and create a better life for their family, my grandfather built a home in the city of Richmond, Virginia. My own father, in turn, built his home across the street from my grandparents' house, and we lived in that home all of the years of our youth. In fact, my former wife and infant daughter and I lived there for a time in the early years of our marriage. And, even after I passed the bar examination in 1960, I located my law office a mere three blocks from the home in which I was raised. So, I had the good fortune of being surrounded by the love and protection of family for my entire childhood and young adulthood.

The term "poverty" is being thrown around so loosely today; it seems to have become the favorite scapegoat for the personal, moral shortcomings of many people. But poverty, in and of itself, is no excuse for one's failure to succeed and to thrive in this world. I grew up during the time of segregation, when black Americans were not permitted to sit in the front of a bus, use the same restrooms, attend the same schools or use the same water fountains and hotels as white Americans. Yet, my family, my teachers, and the people in my community never taught me or my peers to see ourselves as anything less than capable.

Though poor in the economic sense, my parents demanded we children take pride in ourselves, in our achievements and in our home, which they took great care to fill with the refinements of culture: vases of fresh flowers, carpets on the floor, and a piano which my father made sure everyone had the opportunity to learn to play. (To make this possible, my father would pay his colleague at the Southern Aid Life Insurance Company $.10 per lesson—despite the fact that the company never paid my father over $50 a week in his entire life!) As tough as things were for us economically, my father made sure that each week at church, we kids had something to put into the church basket, even if it was no more than a nickel or a couple of pennies. It was a profound lesson in the power of giving that has stayed with me to this day.

I remember when my mother and I would get on the street car one block from my home at the end of the line and, even if the street car was empty, she would tug at me and say, "Let's go sit a little further in the back." Recognizing that, at five years old, I didn't really understand what the words "colored" and "white" meant, she would simply say, "Come, let's sit here and I will explain it to you one day." But that day never came. She never tried to tell me that I had to sit one place or that I had to do something else. Instead, she would always tell me to *know* what was right and to always make certain that I *did* what was right!

The message was no different in school, where all of my teachers and the school's principal took on the responsibility of making certain that we kids dressed properly, that we spoke properly and that we acted properly—in class as well as out! Bear in mind that my elementary school had neither cafeteria nor library. It had no auditorium and the first wooden building was one with outdoor toilets. We did not have regular access to school nurses. Yet no one made excuses for us. To the contrary, like our parents, our teachers had high expectations for us. Despite the odds—as poor children living in a segregated, pre-civil rights society—we were pushed to excel and taught that we could, through personal effort, achieve the American dream. Even the old men in my neighborhood, many of whom could not read or had not finished school, encouraged us to stay in school and get an education. They encouraged us because they had the wisdom to know that education was going to make us whole. That it would make us into people who could contribute to society and open the doors for us to become a valuable part of that society, *even* in a segregated situation.

I am part of the older generation now, and we are charged with the task of successfully instilling in your generation an understanding and appreciation of the travails that have been overcome and what it takes to overcome them. It is a daunting charge. As I look out across the American cultural landscape today, I am reminded of Winston Churchill's description of the Soviet movement across Europe, which he likened to an "iron curtain" descending across the continent. I am left to wonder how we have gone from a generation that, during the depths of segregation, was taught to believe that we could achieve the American dream, to today, where so much emphasis is on self-interest, violence and *mediocrity*.

There are those who say that they cannot succeed because some entity holds them back or because the government is still in the way or the judicial system and state legislatures are still blocking the path; and, to some extent, this may be true. Certainly there can be no doubt that a historic damage has been done to a great number of people in this country by what has been a pattern of neglect and, in some instances, racism and slavery. If you are a young man of color, it would be easy to listen to those friends and peers who tell you that you cannot make it because this is a white world or, if you are poor, because it is a world controlled by the rich, and so on. There will never be a shortage of people who will try to convince you that you have no chance in this society. However, as one who lived through—and rose above—both poverty and segregation, I believe I speak with some authority in saying that poverty, cultural barriers, segregation, or even slavery itself will no longer be a sufficient reason for any person or any child in America to say that success is not attainable. Raised in segregation, the grandson of slaves, I would go on to become the governor of Virginia. You tell me what obstacles cannot be overcome!

The words of Thomas Jefferson that *"all men are created equal"* apply to me and to you and to each and every person in this country! This great promise of America was enshrined in my heart and soul and, ultimately, into my thinking by my mother. And because of her, I never felt that there was anything that I could not achieve. When I was sworn in as governor of Virginia, I concluded my remarks by saying that, "I am a son of Virginia." I said that because I was a product of what Virginia brought to fruition: the *good*, the *bad and* the *ugly*. Whatever and whomever I was sprang forth from here.

When I think back on my childhood, I consider myself lucky to have grown up in the time that I did. That may surprise some people, but looking back, I do not see the ravages of poverty and racism. Instead, I see the wealth of a community of people who lifted me up and pushed me to achieve my best. Our families, our teachers, and our communities taught us to believe in our ability to succeed and the heroes we looked to—men like Martin

Luther King, Jr., Sidney Poitier and Jackie Robinson—joined in the chorus by achieving great success despite overwhelming odds.

Conversely, you are being raised in a culture where the media, which seems to be omnipresent in our lives, produces segments that do not really motivate or challenge you to succeed. Where are the role models who inspire you to be your best? Turn on the network news or open the front page of the paper and you'll find that the turmoil in the Middle East, the fetishes of a possible child killer, and Tom Cruise's lack of a movie deal are all treated with the same gravitas. The employment status of Paris Hilton consistently gets more analysis than the national economy. Right there, you know something is out of kilter.

I am not here to lay blame at the feet of the media—the media is just one arc in a vicious circle of voyeurism. Whose voyeurism came first is really a "chicken and egg" question and of no importance. What is important—and in fact imperative—is that you *become aware* of what goes on in your community and in the world, and that you not be satisfied with the snippets and sound bites that occur in headlines and newsflashes. You must not accept mediocrity! Challenge what you are being told by the pop culture scions leading your generation. *Learn to discern what is real from that which is manufactured by popular media.* Listen to what you hear, think before speaking, and be ready to go in search of deeper understanding.

Each one of you is capable of greatness but, in order to achieve it, you must be willing to let go of the boy and embrace the man. You cannot continue to walk in a crippled state when you are not crippled, stumble about as though you are blind when you are not blind, or appear to be deaf when you are really able to hear. You must instead embrace possibility, work for success, and be satisfied with nothing less than excellence.

Major General Ronald L. Johnson, USA (Ret.)

Major General Ronald L. Johnson, USA (Ret.)

Photo credit: NBA Photos

      Ronald L. Johnson is a retired two-star general and the NBA's senior vice president in charge of referee operations. General Johnson's position with the NBA was created in the wake of a betting scandal that rocked the league's officiating program, and reflected the NBA's desire for a leader possessed of both immense skill and impeccable character.

Raised on Chicago's notorious West Side, General Johnson credits his tough-as-nails high school ROTC instructor for pushing him—hard—to rise above his difficult circumstances. That hard push paid off, and young Ron Johnson was selected to attend the U.S. Military Academy at West Point. Following graduation from West Point, he embarked on a successful military career that spanned 32 years and took him to all parts of the globe including Bosnia, where he was the commander of the 130th Combat Engineering Brigade, and Iraq where, as commanding general of the U.S. Army Corps of Engineers, Gulf Region Division, he was responsible for overseeing $18 billion of reconstruction. In his final command, General Johnson had the distinction of serving as deputy commanding general of the U.S. Army Corps of Engineers, a position that accorded him the status of being the second-highest ranking engineer staff officer in the United States Army.

General Johnson holds several advanced degrees including a master's degree in operations research and systems analysis from Georgia Tech and a master's degree in military strategy from the Army's School of Advanced Military Studies. In addition, he was an Army War College Fellow at the Joint Center for Political and Economic Studies and received executive leadership and national security training at Harvard University, George Washington University, the University of Virginia, Gallup University and the Center of Creative Leadership.

General Johnson is the recipient of numerous awards, including the 2008 Black Engineer Lifetime Achievement Award. He was a 2005 inductee into Georgia Tech's Academy of Distinguished Engineering Alumni and the recipient of the 2003 Black Engineer of the Year Award for Professional Achievement in Government Service. His military decorations include the Distinguished Service Medal (with two Oak Leaf Clusters), the Legion of Merit, the Bronze Star Medal, the Combat Action Badge, the Parachutist Badge and the Air Assault Badge.

Editor's Note

General Ronald L. Johnson grew up in a single-parent household on Chicago's notorious West Side. Like many kids in his neighborhood, he barely knew his father. Indeed, he remembers seeing him only a few times after his father was released from prison. And though he escaped the dangerous West Side streets, his brother and sister were not so lucky: both died too young from the effects of drugs.

But that is Ron Johnson's background; it is not his story. Rather, he saw education, determination and hard work–a "quest for excellence" as he puts it–as his path to a better life. In high school he joined the junior ROTC, where his innate abilities were soon recognized by a "crusty and stubborn retired chief warrant officer who must have seen more in [me] than [I] saw in [myself]." And he saw "opportunities" in high school where others might have found despair. Rather that listening to the taunts of his peers, General Johnson turned those taunts into a resolve to succeed. And succeed he did.

I had the pleasure of spending time with General Johnson one cold December morning at his NBA office in New York City. Though I cannot claim to know him well, I spent enough time with him to be sure of two things: that I am both deeply honored and deeply grateful to have had the chance to get to know him even a little.

And I'm sure of one more thing as well: Ron Johnson knows what it means to be "a better man" because that is what he had to be in order to survive.

I am delighted to introduce you to a man of excellence, compassion, experience and wisdom, Maj. Gen. Ronald L. Johnson.

A Conversation with Maj. Gen. Ronald L. Johnson

KHJ: *When I was doing my research for this interview, I found it interesting–the way that "rebuilding" has been such a big part of what you have done over the course of your career. That makes sense since you are an engineer who was working within the Army Corps of Engineers. But still, just a few years ago you were in charge of $18 billion worth of rebuilding in Iraq, and now you've been brought in to "rebuild" the reputation of the NBA's refereeing operation. So there is a kind of symmetry there and an ability within you to take things or people who are "broken" and move them forward to a better place. So here we are with this book full of all kinds of great advice and experience, but the reality is that, like the referees and like Iraq, some readers are coming to this book from a bad place. Some of them have already made (or will soon make) mistakes that have cost them their reputations or embarrassed their families or violated something they believe in. This interview is for them because, as someone who has seen people struggle in the aftermath of mistakes, I'm sure you know how overwhelmed they can feel by guilt or shame. So I would like young men to hear your thoughts on this idea of redemption–of finding one's way back to where you want to be.*

General Johnson: My first and overriding thought is this: You must have something in your life that is bigger than you, and bigger than any person or thing on this earth, that you can turn to to lift you up. My second thought comes from the Bible–the book of James, chapter 1–it's beautiful. It's my favorite verse and it basically says that there are only three things that are ever happening to you in life: you are either going into a storm, you're in the storm or you're coming out of the storm. But, the scripture continues, no matter where you are, you should be rejoicing because when the storm has ended, you are going to be a much better person. So to be cold, to be wet, to be sad–no one wants that–but if we didn't experience these difficult things, we wouldn't know how to appreciate the good things when they arrive.

KHJ: *That really is the answer, isn't it? But maybe we can break it down a little bit more because, as you know, when you are young and "in the middle of the storm," the journey to redemption can feel nearly impossible. And you see these kids and you just know they're wondering how they'll ever build that bridge back to where they want to be.*

General Johnson: Well, we can't talk about redemption without talking about the notion of grace, and grace tells me that I'm human and I'm bound to make some mistakes. But it also tells me that if I'm prayerful about it, and if I try to live the way God wants me to live, then ultimately I'll be okay. And I really believe that.

And you remember that life really is a marathon: 26 miles, 385 yards. And during a marathon, everybody hits this thing known as "the wall" where you just feel miserable; you feel hopeless; you feel like there's no way you're going to finish it. But if you know life's a marathon and you're out there running, then you know, too, that you can't quit when you hit the wall. You say to yourself, "I'm at the 20-mile point—there are only six miles to go. I've got to keep putting one foot in front of the other." And guys who run marathons, somehow they manage to do that. And it's *very hard*, it's *very difficult*, and it *doesn't* feel good. Eventually, you can see that finish line and it's the greatest feeling in the world. But you need to have some way to visualize where you're at, what you're doing, and what you have ahead of you.

KHJ: *I wonder too if one of those first steps isn't forgiveness. What I mean is the willingness to forgive oneself. It can be a terribly hard thing to do, especially if there is a public element to whatever we've done wrong. But I think it may be a critical first step.*

General Johnson: You're right; and that has certainly been true for me. I know that when something goes wrong in my life—whether my divorce or my son having difficulties—I start with me and say, "Okay, what was it that I did (or what was it that I didn't do) that may have caused this?" For me, it is really hard to try to forgive myself, but I think you're right—you can't just be—you can't move on from a mistake until you can leave it behind. And you can't leave it behind until you forgive yourself . . . or others—people who may have hurt you.

So I think you're absolutely right. But forgiveness takes a couple things. I think sometimes people going through hard times isolate themselves because they're embarrassed, something maybe has been made public. It's like that old thing where you have a hole in your sock and you think everybody sees it. In reality no one knows it's there except you. But relatively speaking, you think everybody sees and notices. And that's how you may feel when you've made a mistake and so you tend to withdraw. You don't want to be around anybody because you really don't want to talk about what you've done or how you're feeling. I've done that. We all have. But what I've found is that the more I open up, the more I discover how mundane my situation was. It is like, "Wow, everybody has problems and lots of people have this particular problem." What you take away is the realization that, "There's nothing wrong with me; this is just the way life is."

This reaching out and talking is the precursor to forgiving yourself, and I don't think it can really happen if you stay isolated.

KHJ: *So we begin with forgiveness. Then what?*

General Johnson: Next is taking responsibility. There is always the side-trip into what "they" did that caused this to happen to me, right? We want to blame someone else. And the truth is that someone else may share in the blame, but you need to own your part. You need to take responsibility for where you are right now. And you need to act on that. If I stick with the marathon analogy, I'd say this: "If you're training to run a marathon, don't hang out with people who are training to be quarter-milers." Stated another way, when you make mistakes, sometimes it's not what you're doing, but it's the people around you and what they're doing. And you may get caught up in what's going on or you may just be a bystander to it; but because of your associations, because you're linked to them–that causes problems. So one of the things you've got to do is still love those people, still treat them with great respect, but get a new group of people to hang out with: people who are going to enhance your life, not rip it down.

My 19-year-old son, *whom I love to death*, has made some choices that I never would have made and that I never expected *him* to make. We've always talked about doing what you've got to do now so that you can do what you want to do later–and not the other way around. Nevertheless, he made some bad choices. He's learning from them, and I'm right there with him, right there by his side. By contrast, when everything went downhill, I asked him, "Where are those 'friends' of yours who were in that car when the police came? I'll tell you where–they disappeared. They went home. They pointed the finger at you. They didn't even call your parents to tell them this was going on. They were out of there."

Those guys weren't truly concerned about him; they were concerned about themselves. So you have to–sometimes you have to come to a hard realization that you need to change the people you associate with–again, a very hard thing to do.

KHJ: *Sitting here with you, hearing you talk about him, hearing the love in your voice–your son is so lucky to have you.*

General Johnson: I believe in him 100 percent. And I can't wait to see the man he turns out to be.

KHJ: *Switching gears just a bit, you know as well as anyone that we all make mistakes. And I think a lot of our mistakes are ones that sort of sneak up on us. We find ourselves there in the moment trying to decide what to do and that's when we tend to make bad decisions. It's just too easy "in the moment" to ignore that tiny voice inside. All of a sudden, we find ourselves heading down the wrong path.*

By contrast, you look at the military or NASA–those organizations plan for trouble! They assume things will go wrong and they plan for it; and as a result they develop a kind of mental discipline in the face of problems. So maybe that is a better way to do things–you pick a few situations: shoplifting, cheating, drugs, et cetera, and then visualize over and over what your response will be. Maybe we'd make fewer dumb decisions over time.

General Johnson: (laughs) You might be right, because in the military, the idea is that you don't want to be trying to decide what to do "in the moment." You want to know ahead of time how to act, so that when the situation arises, you are acting out of habit. You *train your mind* to react a certain way to a particular situation.

If we trained our Soldiers* how to handle things only when they went the way we wanted them to, or the way we hoped they would, and didn't train them to be ready for the bad guy who also has a vote in the way things unfold, that would be unfair to them because they wouldn't know what

---

*While we recognize that the word "soldiers" is not normally capitalized, General Johnson wrote and asked us to please capitalize it in his interview in tribute to the men and women who serve this country so bravely and honorably, often at the cost of their lives. We were delighted to comply with his request.

to do when they came upon a problem. That's the worst kind of on-the-job training, but that is what we set ourselves up for any time we don't think about situations ahead of time. And sure, sometimes we need to make mistakes and we need to get caught because getting caught saves us from getting deeper into whatever trouble we're in. But you don't want to operate that way in general.

KHJ: *Is this what you do? Or have done? Clearly your choices have been mostly very good ones—you would not be where you are if they hadn't.*

General Johnson: I've made some bad choices in my life, of course. We all do. I think I'm doing pretty well now in terms of the kinds of choices I make. But I've reflected on this a lot because when I think about where I came from and how my life could have ended up, and then compare that to where I am now, the only logical explanation that I can find (and I'm an engineer so I tend to want to be logical) is that the man who was my ROTC instructor in high school was an angel. Now, at the time I thought he was the devil! (laughs) I really didn't like him back then. But he saw something in me that I didn't see in myself. I don't know how or why—but he did, and he completely changed the course of my life. So I absolutely believe that there are angels here on earth who are there to help us find our way.

I know how hard life can be. I know what it takes to succeed when the odds are stacked against you and when no one around you—none of your "friends"—want to see you succeed. I often tell a story about a friend of mine. He was from the West Side of Chicago, raised by a single parent, living on welfare. As a kid, he had been robbed several times, and he'd been shot at. But he grew up, and he made his way to West Point—and now he's sitting here in front of you, a two-star general.

KHJ: *Oh, wait a second—you're the "friend"?*

General Johnson: (laughs) I tell this story because I want boys to know what is possible—despite whatever odds they're facing. I want them to *know* what is possible. And when they screw it up, I want them to know that redemption is possible.

KHJ: *If they're still breathing, redemption is still possible.*

General Johnson: Exactly. If they're breathing, it's possible.

169

KHJ: *What one piece of wisdom would you not part with for the world?*

General Johnson: Wow, that is tough because the good thing about wisdom is that it is the only thing I can share and keep at the same time. But, that said, I would say this—and I firmly believe this: I can do anything if I work at it.

KHJ: *Ready for word association?*

General Johnson: Shoot.

KHJ: *Bullies.*

General Johnson: Cowards.

KHJ: *Compassion.*

General Johnson: Two things come to mind. First, a name: Desmond Tutu. Second, is what I like to call the "platinum" rule: Do unto others as you would *like* them to do unto you. By that I mean that you do not simply do unto them what you would *have* them do to you. You go further. You do that something extra—that thing that you would really *like* to have done for you.

KHJ: *Boys don't cry.*

General Johnson: Yes, they do.

KHJ: *Respect for women.*

General Johnson: Absolutely nonnegotiable; gotta have it. We all come from women—our mothers!

Will Heller

Will Heller

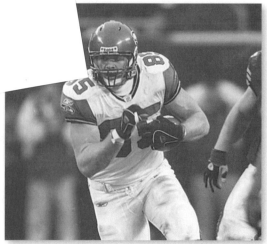

Photo credit: Seattle Seahawks/Corky Trewin

Will Heller is a Seattle Seahawks football player whose path to the NFL was paved with perseverance, grit and a fierce determination. He took up the game late in high school, almost as an afterthought. But his extraordinary mental toughness and indomitable work ethic soon set him apart and, ultimately, made his journey to the NFL possible.

Will graduated from Marist School in Atlanta where he was a standout athlete in both football–winning All-Dekalb County honors–and basketball. Always seeking both an academic and athletic challenge, Will turned down a scholarship offer from Furman University, deciding instead to accept the challenge of trying to make the team at Georgia Tech as a walk-on. He became a scholarship player after his first year, and by his senior year, he was the starting tight end for the Yellow Jackets. At six feet six inches and 265 pounds, he was beginning to get noticed by NFL scouts impressed by his size, his toughness and his devastating blocking ability.

Will graduated with a civil engineering degree from Georgia Tech in 2003, but was not drafted by an NFL team, a decision that many undoubtedly rue to this day. Undeterred, and with his typical determination, Will went to camp with the Tampa Bay Buccaneers as an undrafted free agent and, just as he had at Georgia Tech, made the team, pushing aside some much bigger names to do so. In fact, he was the only undrafted free agent to earn a spot on the Buccaneers' roster that year. After two seasons at Tampa and part of a season with the Miami Dolphins, Will was picked up by the Seattle Seahawks in 2006, where he quickly became a valued member of the team, appearing in every game and upping his game stats with each passing season.

Editor's Note

I first "met" Will Heller through an article I read about him in the Seattle Times. *Written by veteran sports writer Steve Kelley, the article profiled Will following his standout performance in a game against the New York Giants where this supposedly "nonreceiving tight end" caught two touchdown passes.*

Will Heller, so impressive and down to earth on paper, is doubly so in real life. He is exactly as Steve described him, and then some. The trouble for me is that Steve Kelley managed to capture him so well, there is no way to improve on what he did—believe me, I tried.

I called Steve and told him my dilemma. Lucky for me, Steve Kelley is just as easy-going and as gracious as his subject; and he has very generously allowed me to reprint his article here. I do so with gratitude and a sigh of relief:

> Players get branded. Like actors, they are stereotyped into certain roles, stuck in situations that are difficult to escape.
>
> Take Will Heller .... Heller is a blocking tight end. He is the guy who wedges a hole for running back Shaun Alexander on third-and-short. Or protects quarterback Matt Hasselbeck from some ill-intentioned linebacker.
>
> Heller is the football equivalent of a character actor. An almost-anonymous, glamorless figure in a high-visibility game. Even though he wears the same number as Cincinnati's spotlight-seeking Chad Johnson, Heller is no "Ocho Cinco." He is the mute button to Johnson's booming bass. He is the whisper to Ocho Cinco's screams.
>
> "Will's probably not the guy people think about when they think about tight ends," said former Seahawks fullback Mack Strong, who played the game with that same kind of quiet selflessness for 15 seasons. "But he's a heck of a player, and I think Seattle found

another weapon today."

Heller . . . took the hard road to the NFL. He walked on at Georgia Tech. Got a degree in civil engineering. Went undrafted and signed with Tampa Bay in 2003. After two seasons with the Bucs, he split a year with Miami and Tampa Bay before signing with the Seahawks last season.

He did what he was told. Blocked whom he was supposed to block and caught a mere four passes in 2006.

And he was quiet as snowfall.

"He's a beast," said wide receiver Nate Burleson. "He's a former basketball player, so he knows how to position his body. Great hands. Soft-spoken. Doesn't celebrate. Just goes out there and plays ball and does the dirty work."

"Yeah, I have been kind of labeled as a nonreceiving tight end," [Will] said, "But that's how this league works. That's how life is. This was a big day for me [scoring two touchdowns.] It was a lot of fun. I'm glad it worked out the way it did. In this business, that's what you're expected to do when you're a back-up. You're expected to go in there and replace the first guy like there's nothing different."

"It's kind of been my deal. I just come to work. Work hard, do what I'm supposed to and hopefully do it right," he said. "I've always been quiet. But that's not to say I'm not having fun. I'm lovin it."

[This past Sunday,] Will Heller's hard work was rewarded. Good things happened to a good person. . . . Will Heller escaped the stereotype. Will Heller was a star.

I am delighted to introduce one of the most impressive and gracious young men that I've ever had the pleasure to meet, Mr. Will Heller.

A Conversation with Will Heller

KHJ: Steve Kelley, a sports writer for the Seattle Times, *wrote an article about you at the end of last season, and he said, among other things, that you "took the hard road to the NFL." Tell me about that.*

Will: Well, my story starts with basketball, funny enough. My high school went from 7th to 12th grade. Up 'til then, I had always been the best player on the team in basketball. I was pretty talented, I guess, for my age. But once I got into high school, everyone hit their growth spurts—and I didn't. And it was tough there for awhile. So, from about 7th to maybe 10th grade, I went from being a leader on teams to, really, barely making teams. It was hard on me. But one of the best things about my high school was the fact that we had great varsity coaches. We didn't have the most talented athletes [in the county]; but they really drove it into us that with hard work and discipline we could outsmart the other teams—we could outplay them mentally. So it was a whole team effort—everyone had a role and a job to do. And it worked.

KHJ: So then, I'm curious. What made you decide to switch over to football?

Will: I wish I could tell you that there was something that led me in that direction or some great story about how I ended up there. But the truth of the matter is that I joined the football team to make friends. That's it. Basketball was the big sport at our high school back then, and that was what I really wanted to be good at. Football was just a way to get to know people. But I was having trouble keeping up in basketball. Everyone was getting taller and stronger and I just wasn't. I thought about quitting football a few times to really try and focus on basketball; but my friends talked me into sticking with it.

The odd thing is, in the end, the thing that I think really helped me succeed in football actually came from my experience playing basketball. Like I said, we had great coaches, and one coach in particular . . . he talked so much about how God gives each person a pool of talent and how some people have a much larger pool than others. But, he said that it's never about how big your pool of talent is; it's what you do with it.

Another big inspiration for me was a guy who went to my high school named Matt Harpring, who plays now in the NBA. I was in 7th grade when he was a senior. But our stories are very similar in that, as a junior in high school, he didn't even start on the basketball team. Then, his senior year, he shot up six inches, became a starter, got a scholarship to play at Georgia Tech and ended up 15th overall in the NBA draft. What I admired about him was the fact that he was such a hard worker and had so much self-discipline—and not just as a starter. He was that way even when he was spending most of his time on the bench. He really bought into what our coaches had taught him and he utilized his pool of talent, I think, to its fullest. So, when his time came and he had the chance to start, all those skills he'd worked so hard to develop—they just took him through the roof!

I've just always found inspiration in the way he approached what he was trying to do with his whole heart. And my story played out a lot like his: I think I was maybe, five foot five in 8th grade, and I had to work twice as hard just so that I could hold my own against guys much bigger than me. But by 10th grade, I shot up to six-four.

KHJ: Once you hit that growth spurt, things must have really taken off.

Will: (laughs) Not really. That's where the similarities between me and Matt Harpring end! After high school I got a recruiting letter from some Division II schools saying they might be interested in me. But I didn't get any Division I offers. Again, just like in high school, I looked at playing football in college as a way to make friends. It was a way to continue to play and get a great education. Two or three of my friends were offered scholarships to play at Georgia Tech, and because the Tech [recruiters] were at our games a lot, they ended up offering me a "preferred walk-on" spot, which basically means you come in with the advantage that they know who you are, but not much beyond that.

In the back of my mind, I didn't know if I could compete at a Division I school. I didn't know if I could make it work at that level. But the whole time, my friends were telling me, "You can do it; you've got the size." And the other thing they kept saying and emphasizing, they'd say, "You've got the heart." I wasn't convinced, but they kept pushing me and telling me I could do it.

We worked *so hard* that summer and got ourselves in great shape. I went into training camp at Tech and I realized immediately that I *could* compete at this level. I had a lot to learn, but the discipline we built up in ourselves in high school really carried over. I saw again how that mental toughness our coaches had drilled into us in high school really set us apart and allowed us to compete with this very talented pool of players.

Not to say [those players] didn't work hard! I don't mean that. But so many times it seemed like guys would hit that first or second roadblock and they'd say, "Forget it."

KHJ: *So the mental toughness you think made a difference?*

Will: Absolutely. It made *the* difference. It was the same story again going into the NFL. I was a starter my senior year in college–and again, I wasn't a star by any means. But all of a sudden in my senior year, a couple of teams started asking, "Who is this guy? He's got some size and skill." I wasn't drafted. Instead, just like before, I was a walk-on and made it onto the team that way.

KHJ: *It sounds like you were underestimated a lot.*

Will: Yeah, I guess so.

KHJ: *Clearly, there is an element of that–of having the chance to go in and prove yourself–that you enjoy. You really rise to the challenge. But I imagine there were also some very tough moments–some low points where you had to dig deep. And, obviously, you did that. You found a way through it.*

Will: For me, when I hit those low points, the only satisfaction I could find–the only way I could find to feel better about myself–was to go to work, go out on the field and run. When you're in a position where you're not as talented as the guys around you, all you can lean on in the back of your mind is, "I'm going to be better prepared than them. And I'm going to be in better shape: stronger, smarter, faster." And how I do that is I tell myself I have to be doing more today than they are. That is the only way I'm going to be able to compete at this level against this talent. I will flat outwork them! So when I would get down–and there are constantly ups and downs—I think there are more downs, maybe, when you're not as talented because, well, I don't know, but I think it just shows up more often—I lean on my work ethic. The minute I feel myself getting down, I go and work harder. I keep falling back on that. It's like this backbone that you always have.

KHJ: *For all the things we can't control (talent, coach's choices, et cetera), we almost always have control over what we do and how hard we're willing to work.*

Will: Yeah, exactly. And like I said, I'm hard on myself. But, when you screw up or when you have a bad day, you want to at least be able to say you gave it everything you had. If you can say, "I had a rough day or a rough week, but I did all I could to be prepared for it," you feel better than if you have to say, "I had a bad day and I didn't do all I could have. I didn't work out as hard as I could have or run the plays as well as I could have in practice," or whatever.

KHJ: *You must be having more good days than bad because I read somewhere that you recently signed a two-year contract with the Seahawks. After all the hard work and the ups and downs, you've finally arrived!*

Will: I don't think I can ever—as long as I'm playing—I don't think I would ever admit to myself that I've "arrived." It's just—as soon as you say, "Alright! I'm here. I've done it," I think you fall backwards. I love it here. But when you're in a position like me, you try to just hang on as long as you can.

KHJ: *What do you mean "in a position like me"?*

Will: When you're not a highly paid player or a high draft pick, there's really no obligation from the franchise's standpoint to keep you. So you're always fighting for your life to keep your position. If you can fight long enough, the opportunity's going to come because there are so few players per team, and there are injuries, trades or whatever. And NFL careers are made and broken by that *one* opportunity that you get. So at this level, it is the climax of all the preparation you've been doing since you were a kid—it all culminates in this one opportunity that you may get.

The one thing I've learned is, don't *ever* sell yourself short. You never know how far you might go. I never thought I'd be where I am now; but now that I'm here I figure, why not try to start? And once you start, why not try to be the best starter in your division? And once you're that, why not try to be the best starter in the NFC?

KHJ: *What is something most people don't know about being a professional football player?*

Will: Well, there is a certain "celebrity" aspect to professional sports. It's so glamorized by television. But if anyone could spend two weeks in the locker room, you'd see—it's the same game you've been playing since you were six. It is the *same* thing, it's just these guys are *really* good at it. I certainly don't think of myself as a celebrity. But I don't think of the star players as celebrities either. I mean, some of them get involved in commercials and Campbell's soup ads or whatever—and that's fine. But when we're at work and playing the game, that's all there is.

KHJ: *Okay, and now for everyone who has ever dreamed of playing in the NFL, tell me, what's the best thing about your job?*

Will: One of the things that is so appealing and fun to me happens during game week. Let's say you're playing the Falcons on Sunday. You go in Monday, and the analysts start talking and there's all this hoopla. They're all saying, "This team's not gonna win because so-and-so is hurt," or "This team's stronger on defense," or whatever. Tuesday it keeps building up. Wednesday it keeps building up. By Thursday, everybody thinks they've got it figured out—they "know" who's gonna win. Sunday is a huge spectacle —vendors, cheerleaders, thousands of people screaming—just complete chaos. And amidst all this nonsense, all that matters at any given point in time is the one play in front of me. All that matters is whether I can do my job—can I do my job against that guy across from me? Because, if I do my job each time, and the guy next to me does his job each time, and on down the line, *that* is what's going to determine the outcome. *That's* what determines who wins or loses! Not the [analysts] in the booth. So you ignore what they're saying and do your job.

It's just so simple. You've got 11 guys on the field, and every one of you just has to do your job on every single play. If you do that, it doesn't really matter what else is going on in that stadium or what people have said. I really get a lot of satisfaction out of that.

KHJ: *I can imagine! You know, listening to your story, I'm not sure I'm buying this idea that you never got back to being a stand-out player, like when you were young.*

Will: (laughs)

KHJ: *But, you're a lot bigger than me so I'm not going to argue with you. So then, assuming for the sake of argument that it's true, I wonder, do you miss it? Do you miss being a star player?*

Will: Actually, no. I've always had respect for the guys who found a way to be helpful to the team—even though they weren't the stars and weren't going to be.

KHJ: *What appealed to you?*

Will: Kind of the blue-collar nature of it, I guess. It's always been satisfying to me, ironically, to help a team win and maybe not get in the limelight. I mean, you want to be recognized for your effort, but not that spotlight kind of recognition. They just go out there and get the job done—no hoopla.

KHJ: *That sounds sort of John Wayne-esque to me. You know—like the great unsung hero.*

Will: Yeah, I guess it does. But I've always enjoyed that role and I've looked up to the guys who have that role. And the great thing about our high school program was that from the coaches down, they taught us to embrace that role and they always let us feel the importance of it. I saw the respect they had for those guys and I guess I wanted to be "that guy" in their eyes.

KHJ: *That seems to me to be a rare quality—to not need or crave the spotlight.*

Will: I don't know if it is just my personality, but it is really satisfying to me to have to work that hard to earn something. And I have nothing against people who are so talented that they start each game and are the stars on the field. That's great. But there's something to be said for going into a training camp with guys who are maybe more objectively talented than you and coming away with the job.

KHJ: *Will, it has been great talking with you—I really mean that. I'm just going to put you through a little word association before I let you go.*

Will: Fair enough.

KHJ: *Okay, here we go. Bullies.*

Will: Weak.

KHJ: *Compassion.*

Will: Important.

KHJ: *Respect for women.*

Will: Very important.

KHJ: *Boys don't cry.*

Will: Yes, they do.

Michael Bantom

Michael Bantom

Photo credit: Stuart O'Sullivan

Mike Bantom is a former professional basketball player and a senior executive with the National Basketball Association. A four-year starter at St. Joseph's College, Mike was selected to play on the 1972 Olympic Basketball team in his junior year. The team ultimately won a silver medal following a controversial loss to the Soviet Union.

Mike averaged 20 points and 13 rebounds per game during his college career and graduated from St. Joe's as second all-time in rebounds and second overall in points scored. He was drafted in the first round (eighth pick, eighth overall) by the Phoenix Suns and was named to the All-Rookie team at the end of his first season. He went on to play in the NBA for another nine years with the Suns, the Seattle SuperSonics, the New York Nets, the Indiana Pacers and the Philadelphia 76ers, with whom he enjoyed a trip to the finals in 1982. He ended his NBA career in 1982 with 8,568 total points, 4,517 total rebounds and 1,623 assists. He then went on to play another seven years of professional basketball in Italy.

Mike was inducted into St. Joseph's Athletics Hall of Fame in 2000. The college retired his jersey number (#44) in 2003–only the third number retired in the school's history at the time.

Following his retirement from professional basketball, Mike embarked on a career as an NBA executive. He served as licensing manager for NBA International and as the NBA's international director of marketing programs before taking on his current role as the NBA's senior vice president of player development.

Editor's Note

Mike Bantom was one of the first gentlemen I interviewed for this book, and I have to say it was a genuine privilege to spend time with him. We met at NBA headquarters in New York City, an office that buzzes with so much activity and star power that it's hard not to get caught up in the excitement. In the midst of it all is Mike Bantom, the calm in the storm and the NBA's vice president of player development.

I was interested in talking to Mike because a big part of his job involves working with each and every rookie player in the NBA. He is there as a guide, father, or mentor—whatever is needed—as these young men navigate their way through their first year as professional ball players and as young men out in the world on their own. What that means, if you're a basketball fan, is that every single player you know, from Dwayne Wade to Michael Jordan, knows Mike. More importantly, he is the one who the young players come to for advice and help not because it's his "job," but because they know that this is a man whose wisdom and experience they can trust. And so can you.

A wise man indeed, it is my pleasure to introduce Mr. Mike Bantom.

A Conversation with Mike Bantom

KHJ: Tell me what it was like for you growing up in Philadelphia in the 1960s and 1970s.

Mike: I grew up in a fairly rough neighborhood. My parents divorced when I was young, and my sisters and I lived with my mother. It was a tremendous struggle for her and she had to work incredibly hard to provide for us. Because of the demands placed on her life, I had a lot of unsupervised time when I was a kid. The trouble was—well, it was a lot of things—but one thing was that there weren't a lot of positive male role models for young African-Americans where I grew up. You saw a handful of black baseball players on TV and in the news who were successful and making money and you saw a lot of "hustlers" in your neighborhood. That was it. In fact, I can't think of one black male professional who lived in my neighborhood or who got a lot of exposure on television or in the media—or anywhere else for that matter. So I had a very limited view of who I could become when I was young. Fortunately for me, basketball came along.

I didn't play organized ball until I was a junior in high school, and then I was the last man on the varsity team, so I didn't play much! But the summer between my junior and senior years I got passionate about the game and worked hard at getting better. I didn't do it with a goal in mind of playing in college or in the NBA. I did it because I loved the game and I wanted to see how good I could get at it. In one year, I went from being an unknown benchwarmer at a local Catholic high school to being one of only five players chosen for the all-city team in Philadelphia. I was being sought after by colleges in the eastern half of the United States, including all of the Ivy League schools; but, for whatever reason, I decided to go to St. Joseph's College rather than Penn State or Princeton. I guess I felt a sense of loyalty to the team that came after me first. In my junior year at St. Joe's, I was selected to play on the 1972 U.S. Olympic basketball team and, at the end of my senior year, I was the eighth player drafted in the first round to play for the Phoenix Suns. I went on to play professionally for the next 16 years.

KHJ: That's an incredible trajectory—from benchwarmer to the NBA! What comes to mind when you think back on the experiences you had as a college player and the early years in the NBA?

Mike: It was an incredible time in my life, obviously, and I'm extremely grateful for it. I had the opportunity to do things and experience things that I could not have even dreamed of as a kid. But in truth, probably the most important thing that happened to me, happened during my sophomore year in college when I signed up for an elective course in philosophy. At that point, I had gone to Catholic school my entire life—and I mean all the way from first grade to twelfth grade. Now I was an English major at a Catholic college! I'd had questions about my faith, like most young people do, but I hadn't done much with them—hadn't pursued answers.

This course opened my eyes to the fact that the world was full of people with different philosophies about life, different religions, and different ways of relating to the world. By the end of that semester, I knew that I could no longer be "Catholic" simply because that is what had been handed to me. Instead, I had to find a way in life that I could call my own. The trick was figuring out what that meant. So that's what I set out to do, and throughout the remainder of my college years and my first years in the NBA, I spent most of my spare time reading books that pushed me to redefine who I was as a person.

I read everything from Buddhism to Confucianism to the Sutras of the Yogis. In a real way, I was on two simultaneous journeys—one in the world of basketball and the other in the equally important world of self-discovery. And slowly, over the course of months and years, I started figuring out how I wanted to live, how I could blend these two parts of myself into one.

KHJ: Can you tell me what you finally arrived at as your own philosophy?

Mike: I settled on three basic tenets that I felt were critical to how I wanted to live my life. First, I had to believe in a higher power and I had to trust that power. That was essential. Second, I had to be true to myself. If I wasn't true to myself, then the rest was just talk. And third, I had to think and act in a way that was true to my new understanding about how this world works. Specifically, I believed then, as I believe now, that a divine interconnectedness exists between all living things, and that everything we do, large or small, has a consequence. The way we treat the world, the way we treat other people, the way we *think*–they all have an impact on you and the world around you. Whether you see that impact immediately or not, it's there. If you're putting negative stuff out into the world, it will come back to you eventually. On the other hand, if you are careful about what you do and what you think, you can have a very positive effect on the people and things around you.

KHJ: So, you're saying we create our own happiness (or unhappiness)?

Mike: More than that, really. It's not just about finding a way to be happy, though that's certainly an important part of it. It is about being active in the course and design of your life. I'd be willing to bet that most of the people writing for this book–and most of the people who are really successful in this world–understand that they are co-creators of their lives along with some kind of a higher power. Some people don't share this belief and yet they seem to do great things. But most, I think, feel this co-creativeness and know that their success comes from a larger place. They don't harbor any misconceived notion that they are somehow uniquely blessed. What *is* unique about them, however, is their ability to trust in a higher power and work *with* it, instead of against it. It took me a while to come to that understanding and make it part of my own life. But now, I absolutely trust in that higher power and whenever I'm severely challenged or when there are obstacles in my way, I don't feel overwhelmed.

KHJ: Was getting this job part of that process?

Mike: It was. Around the time my NBA career was coming to an end, I had to reassess where I was in my life. I had to ask myself, "What are you going to do? Who are you going to be?" And that's when I decided that I was really just going to focus on trying to be the best *person* I could be–and that meant to my ex-wife, to my children, to whomever I encountered. Whatever my choice of careers was going to be, I was going to be as good as I could be in that as well. And, regardless of the outcome, that was going to be enough for me. I stopped fretting about all the other things that I had been fretting about, and instead, put my beliefs into practice. What did that mean? It meant that I took the steps I could take to begin to make things happen–polishing my resume, sending out letters–having faith that the things that I needed would come my way. And they did. I came to work for the NBA in 1989 and, throughout the course of my career, the right doors have opened for me time and time again. I haven't looked back since. And I haven't had any more doubts about this higher power and how it moves in our world.

KHJ: Obviously, your success in the NBA organization didn't happen all at once. You worked at it over the course of years. But today it seems as if so much is geared toward what is quick and easy.

Mike: Absolutely. Young men today are growing up in a culture that tells them everything has to be big–big money, big celebrity, big influence. The attitude is, "I want it and I want it now!" But nothing *real* happens like that! Anything of lasting value takes time. You look at a Sidney Poitier and then at the "overnight sensations" you see in the music or entertainment industry. What you want, what you *really* want as a person, is going to be achieved by taking the route that Sidney Poitier took. He worked at his craft. He made choices that helped him grow not only as an actor, but as a person, and today, he is one of the most admired and respected actors in the world. Yet, as a young man, you're more likely to be attracted to the guy with the overnight success because that's the guy with the Rolls-Royce and the "bling-bling," surrounded by beautiful women. You're going to say to yourself, "That's what I want!" But that's *not* really what you want in the long run. What you want is *the ability to create those things for yourself* and to *create the life* that you want.

Of course we need money to survive, and we want to be able to move beyond our basic needs and find ourselves in a position where we can afford to have the things that we want. But it is too easy I think, especially as men, to make the mistake of equating what we do for a living with who we are as people. We are not our jobs. I loved being a basketball player, and yet, it is not who I was. A job will be something that you do, and you will have to learn certain things in order to do it well. But it is not who you are as a person. And *who you are* as a person deserves at least as much attention as *what you do* at your job. You have to find a way to bring both parts of yourself together because at the end of the day, I don't care how flashy your life may seem, if you haven't done the internal work first, there's not going to be any substance to it and I guarantee you're going to come to regret that.

You hear celebrities talk about this all the time. They get to a certain point and then they start singing and rapping about how there has to be more to their life than just material comforts. What they're looking for is that feeling that they are connected to something. They need to feel that there is more to their existence than just piling up that bank account. When

I started in the NBA, I made the mistake of working just for the "stuff" my playing brought me. I wasn't feeling fulfilled even though all of my friends, and 99 percent of the young black men in the country, would have changed places with me in a heartbeat. I was in the NBA, I still had two or three years guaranteed contract, I was playing well–and most people would have said, "What the hell have you got to be unhappy about?" But I wasn't happy. I had gotten caught up being a young professional basketball player and I was doing everything that was being presented to me–women, partying, having fun. I wasn't doing anything that was illegal. But it wasn't truly fulfilling. I didn't feel like I was doing anything meaningful with my life. So I had to kind of take a step back and decide whether I wanted to continue playing professional basketball. Ultimately, the answer was "yes," but I had to adopt a completely different outlook on my life, both on and off the court. I began to treat my job as a player with the same sense of responsibility as I would a job in any other profession. I worked hard. I got married. I had kids. And I continued to read and learn and stretch myself as a person. Then, and only then, did my life start to make sense and have real meaning.

I see the same thing when our rookies come in each year. We spend a week with them doing a lot of training and examining a whole host of issues, including the kinds of issues I'm talking about here. But we also have a chance within that week to eat with our new players, talk to them, and spend time with them. Every year, by the end of that week, I can tell you who is here for the long run and who is going to have problems if they don't change real quick. It's that obvious! There are some guys who are really grounded and then there are some guys who are just flying high on their talent. That's where my staff and I step in. We come together after that week and we say, "Who do we think is going to be okay and who do we really need to focus on before he does damage to himself or his career?"

KHJ: You talked about having "the ability to create the life that you want." How do you develop that within yourself?

Mike: You do it through hard work and through a lot of sacrifice and a lot of self-discovery. Every day you have to be willing to do the work it takes to find out a little bit more about life and about the world–and about your own strengths and weaknesses. You work at it until it becomes a habit, so that when you do fall short or you don't get something right, you've got the discipline you need to come back the next day and continue to push forward. Yes, it's a challenge and a struggle to gain the confidence and the control in your life that you need, but I promise you it will come. You'll eventually get it. You'll eventually gain the control that you want. You'll eventually be able to do the things you want to do. But it requires perseverance because there will be many times when you just want to give up and many opportunities to doubt whether you can succeed at what you are doing or not.

KHJ: If you had the chance to give young men today one piece of advice—and you could be guaranteed they would accept it without question—what would it be?

Mike: Without question? Now that's some magic!

If I had the chance to talk to a young man and give him one piece of advice? I don't say this unless I really know the kid, but I would tell him to pray. The reason I don't often say that people should pray is because "prayer" is a hot-button word. It means different things to different people, and it makes a lot of people uncomfortable. But that is what I would tell him to do because that is what I think you *have* to do. And once you understand what prayer is, and what it can be, then that other stuff falls away. So when I talk about "finding out who you are" and "finding your true self," what I'm really saying, but in a different way, is to pray. I pray before I give an interview, I pray before meetings, I pray before I speak with anybody, and before I give a presentation. I do it because I have to get in touch with who I am and what it is that I know. Because if I'm not connected to that higher power then there's no telling what I'm going to say or do! But when I have prayed, I know I will be okay. I trust that.

There is so much that you have to learn in this life! You need to be open to that fact and to the fact that there are people here to assist you. No matter what you ultimately do in your life, whether you're a banker or a doctor or a ball player, the only way you will prosper and have a future is if you continue to grow and educate yourself. During one of our training sessions with the rookies, we bring in a couple of experienced players and we get a dialogue going. We're talking about some of the guys who are really successful superstar players who come and tell the rookies about how, when they were starting out, they thought they didn't need anybody telling them what to do and they weren't going to need our guidance–a pretty typical attitude for a lot of young men. But then they tell them how wrong they were! These superstars let them know, "You can go another route, but son, you are in for a rude awakening!"

We each are a very small element in this universe. But this higher power—a divine power—exists within each one of us and works for our benefit. It works for my good and for your good, just as it does for every other living thing. If you move with it, you have all the power you need to make things happen and to make things go forward in a positive direction in your life. I'm living proof of that.

KHJ: I'd like to end with a short word association, starting with compassion.

Mike: Love. Oneness.

KHJ: Boys don't cry.

Mike: Fallacy.

KHJ: Bullies.

Mike: Ignorant about themselves.

KHJ: Respect for women.

Mike: A necessity.

The Honorable Harry L. Carrico

The Honorable Harry L. Carrico

Photo credit: Tom Trenz/The Supreme Court of Virginia

Harry L. Carrico is the former chief justice of the Supreme Court of Virginia and the longest serving Supreme Court justice in the state's history. His well-reasoned opinions and the unparalleled dedication he brought to his work earned him the respect and admiration of the national legal community, a respect that is reflected in the numerous awards bearing his name, including the Harry L. Carrico Outstanding Career Service Award given by the Judicial Council of Virginia, the Harry L. Carrico Award for Judicial Innovation given by the National Center for State Courts, and the Virginia State Bar's Harry L. Carrico Professionalism Award. Justice Carrico has received honorary degrees from the College of William and Mary, the George Washington University, the University of Richmond and Shenandoah University. He is also the recipient of countless individual awards including Order of the Coif, the Outstanding Virginian Award, the National 4-H Alumni Award and the VMI Public Service Award.

In 1987, the Virginia State Bar instituted the Harry L. Carrico Professionalism Course, a mandatory course for all new Virginia attorneys, which focuses on the Virginia Rules of Professional Conduct and the general ethical obligations an attorney owes to a client, the courts and society at large. The University of Richmond holds its annual Harry L. Carrico Moot Court Competition in his honor.

The Hon. Harry L. Carrico currently serves both as senior justice on the Virginia Supreme Court and as the visiting professor of law and civic engagement at the University of Richmond.

Editor's Note

I had the pleasure of clerking for Harry Carrico for two years following my graduation from law school. He was the chief justice of the Virginia Supreme Court at that time and I felt alternately honored and overwhelmed by the opportunity to serve as his law clerk. At age 25, I marveled at his extraordinary abilities, not the least of which, in my mind, was his strict adherence to a daunting workday routine.

Every morning he got up at 5:00 a.m., rode his bike 10-15 miles for exercise and arrived at work by 7:15. He never closed up shop before 6:30, unless he was traveling. (Speaking of which, I am convinced the man has driven every highway, by-way and back road across the state of Virginia.) He rarely took an entire weekend off, though he did take up rollerblading at my invitation.

Did I mention he was seventy-five years old at the time?

Above every other quality he possessed—and there are many—what stands out most in my mind is his decency. He was and is the most decent person I've ever met. As chief justice, he obviously was in a position of considerable authority and responsibility. When mistakes happened, as they inevitably do, it would have been easy—understandable even—for him to have become upset. After all, the buck ultimately stopped with him, regardless of who was actually at fault, and the consequence of errors at this level of jurisprudence could be serious. Yet he always remained calm. He never yelled or raised his voice in anger; he never excoriated whoever was to blame. He simply acknowledged the problem and then went about finding solutions. It was, I believe, his way of holding fast to "civility." According to Justice Carrico, this "all-but-forgotten" term, as he calls it, is the cornerstone of a good and just society. It is the thing without which we descend into an abyss of vulgarity and self-satisfaction. Civility, which combines both grace and good manners, is an outward manifestation of the notion that, regardless of circumstance, we must continue to treat one another with respect.

Now in his 90s, Justice Carrico continues to work part-time at the Virginia Supreme Court, in addition to taking on a professorship at the

University of Richmond. Suffice it to say that even now we see no signs of him slowing down. Lucky for me, he did slow down long enough to write the following essay on—what else—civility.

I'm honored to introduce the man who will forever be "the Chief" in my eyes, the Honorable Harry L. Carrico.

Civility

What ever happened to civility? "Civility" is one of the gentlest words in the English language, yet it and its synonym "courtesy" have been all but forgotten in the hurry-up world we live in today.

In trying to find an answer to the question, "What ever happened to civility," I came across a delightful little book. It is titled *Rules of Civility*, and it contains 110 wonderful precepts that George Washington copied into a notebook while still a teenager and kept with him all his life, guiding him in war and peace.

Several of the precepts are pertinent to the points I want to make in this discussion. They read as follows:

> *Every action done in company ought to be done with some sign of respect to those that are present.*
>
> *Use no reproachful language against any one, neither curse nor revile.*
>
> *Utter not base and frivolous things among grave and learn'd men, nor very difficult questions or subjects among the ignorant, or things hard to be believed.*
>
> *Speak not injurious words neither in jest nor earnest; scoff at none although they give occasion.*
>
> *Be not [obstinate] but friendly and courteous, the first to salute, hear, and answer. Be not pensive when it's time to converse.*
>
> *Think before you speak, pronounce not imperfectly, nor bring out your words too hastily, but orderly, distinctly.*

While George Washington thought it necessary to have the precepts to guide one's conduct more than 250 years ago, they are even more necessary today because incivility has invaded every phase of our daily lives. We encounter it at every turn, from a visit to the corner grocery to a debate between candidates for public office.

Every day, we see motorists running red lights, refusing to give turn signals, and failing to yield the right-of-way to pedestrians in marked crosswalks. They are violating the law, of course, but they are also violating the basic rules of common courtesy.

Furthermore, it is most distressing to hear politicians berating one another so harshly in an election campaign. Virginia has experienced bitter political campaigns where it seemed commonplace for one candidate to berate the other rather than debate the substantive issues. Unfortunately, we see this same lack of political civility in our presidential campaigns where too often *ad hominem* attacks substitute for thoughtful dialogue.

But this is not something of recent origin in American politics. In fact, the most tragic instance occurred more than 200 years ago and resulted in the killing of a prominent American by an equally well-known adversary. In 1804, Aaron Burr was a candidate for the office of governor of New York, and Alexander Hamilton was bitterly opposed to Burr's candidacy. A newspaper reported that at a dinner party in Albany, New York, Hamilton had said that Burr was "a dangerous man" and expressed "a still more despicable opinion" of Burr. When Burr read the newspaper article, he asked Hamilton for an explanation of his remarks, indicating a willingness to resolve the matter peacefully by Hamilton retracting his words, disavowing them, or apologizing for them.

A little civility on Hamilton's part might have gone a long way and saved his life, but Burr found Hamilton's replies evasive and threw down the gauntlet. Hamilton accepted the challenge, and on July 11, 1804, the two met in a duel with pistols on the New Jersey shore of the Hudson River. Hamilton's shot went askew, but Burr's hit its mark and severely injured Hamilton. He succumbed the next day. The one shot not only terminated Hamilton's life but also ended Burr's political career; he would be tried later for treason.

Since then, praise be, dueling has been outlawed, but character assassination has not. Indeed, it seems to be the source today of great financial reward. We hear of media commentators who are paid million-dollar salaries just for reporting slanderous stories about innocent people. However, one radio commentator spouted something about the Rutgers University women's basketball team that was too disgusting for even his network to swallow, and it fired him. Even so, there are those who defend him, who think his punishment was too harsh. But one can be a staunch supporter of the First Amendment right to free speech yet applaud the network's action in this case.

I am especially concerned about the decline of civility in my own profession –the legal profession. We are told in a report prepared for the Seventh Circuit Court of Appeals that attorneys are now more than ever developing and employing rude, disrespectful, and generally ill-mannered tactics in dealing with opposing counsel as well as litigants, witnesses, judges, and court personnel.

While I do not think the problem is as severe in Virginia as it might be elsewhere, I have seen enough here to be convinced that the Virginia Bar needs to experience a rebirth of civility, a return to courtesy. Indeed, the Supreme Court of Virginia considered the problem serious enough to require that the oath to be taken by every attorney admitted to practice in Virginia shall include a pledge obligating the admittees to conduct themselves courteously in the practice of law.

So, now, lawyer courtesy is more than an inspirational goal in Virginia; it is a solemn obligation that lawyers in Virginia act with civility toward one another, toward the courts, and toward everyone else with whom they have professional contact.

But the need for civility is not limited to the legal profession–not by a long shot! Civility is the duty of every person, as demonstrated in the following magnificent quotation from remarks of Associate Justice Anthony Kennedy of the Supreme Court of the United States:

> *Civility is the mark of an accomplished and superb professional, but it is even more than this. It is an end in itself. Civility has deep roots in the idea of respect for the individual. We are civil to each other because we respect one another's human aspirations and equal standing in a democratic society. We must restore civility to every part of our legal system and public discourse. Civility defines our common cause in advancing the rule of law. Freedom may be born in protest, but it survives in civility.*

In the effort to restore civility to all of society, the focus should be upon you, the young people of America, for you are our best hope for the future. And if the Rules of Civility that George Washington copied into a notebook as a teenager are what helped make him the great man he became, they can be a wonderful guide for you also. And so I close with George Washington's 110th and final precept–the polestar of a return to civility. It is the most challenging precept of all:

> *Labour to keep alive in your breast that little spark of celestial fire called conscience.*

Tavis Smiley

Tavis Smiley

Photo credit: Kevin Foley

Tavis Smiley is a radio and television commentator, the best-selling author of more than a dozen books, winner of 12 NAACP awards and the founder of the Tavis Smiley Foundation, whose mission is "to enlighten, encourage and empower Black youth." From 1996-2008, he offered political commentary twice weekly on the *Tom Joyner Morning Show*. He hosts a late-night television talk show, *Tavis Smiley*, on PBS, and his radio show, *The Tavis Smiley Show*, is distributed by Public Radio International (PRI), thus making him the first American ever to simultaneously host signature talk shows on both public television and public radio.

Over the course of his career, Tavis has interviewed dignitaries and world leaders, legends from the worlds of sports and music, and virtually every "A-list" celebrity you can think of. In 2000, he traveled with U2 frontman Bono, legendary music producer Quincy Jones, Live Aid creator Bob Geldof and others in a successful effort to garner Pope John Paul II's support for a plan to persuade the world's industrialized nations to forgive much of the debt owed by the world's poorest nations. In 2004, Texas Southern University honored him by establishing the Tavis Smiley School of Communications and the Tavis Smiley Center for Professional Media Studies. In November of 2006, he co-hosted the groundbreaking ceremony for the Martin Luther King, Jr., Memorial in Washington, D.C. He also moderated two nationally televised presidential debates in 2007.

The recipient of numerous awards and honorary doctoral degrees, Tavis has been featured in countless national publications including *Newsweek, Time, USA Today,* the *New York Daily News,* the *Washington Post* and *Vanity Fair* (which inducted him into its hall of fame).

Editor's Note

I first got to know Tavis Smiley by reading his autobiography, What I Know for Sure: My Story of Growing Up in America, *a moving portrait of what it was like for him growing up poor and black in the 1960s and 1970s. Raised near Grissom Air Force Base in Indiana, where his father was stationed, Tavis attended the local public school where he was the only black student in his class. In his book, he talks about the ways in which this made him feel like an outsider. Yet, Tavis says, he also felt as though he was living Dr. Martin Luther King, Jr.'s dream because his teachers and friends, all of whom were white, judged him "not by the color of [his] skin but by the content of [his] character."* By his senior year, he was editor of the yearbook, class president and was voted Most Likely to Succeed—a prescient accolade if there ever was one!*

As an adult, Tavis has worked tirelessly on behalf of the black community through endeavors such as The Tavis Smiley Foundation, The Covenant with Black America, and the State of the Black Union, to name just a few. Like Dr. Martin Luther King, Jr., Tavis' ability to work for and on behalf of the black community, while extending an open hand to the white community, is one of the qualities that has enabled him to be such a powerful catalyst for positive change.

I was fortunate to have the chance to talk with him about some of what he "knows for sure," and especially what he says he learned recently about the high price of profanity.

I'm proud to introduce to you the remarkable Mr. Tavis Smiley.

---

*Tavis Smiley, *What I Know for Sure: My Story of Growing Up in America* (New York: Doubleday, 2006), 98.

A Conversation with Tavis Smiley

KHJ: *I'd like to start with a quote from your book,* What I Know for Sure: My Story of Growing Up in America, *which I've read twice now, by the way. I loved it! The book tells the story of your life and, on page 101, you reiterate one of life's great truths, and that is this: "View yourself as a winner, and you become a winner." When I read that statement it struck me because, in some ways, this book is exploring the flip-side of that. In other words, so much of popular culture bombards young men with such a strange and shallow view of what it means to be a man that it makes it challenging for them to view themselves as "winners." When you look at things like movies, video games, music videos and song lyrics, very often you find that the quintessential male is portrayed as a sort of hyper-sexual, self-aggrandizing badass.*

Because you work in television and radio, I'm curious to know what advice you have for young men that might help them be more savvy consumers of that kind of media.

Tavis: I think the most important thing that I can share in that regard is how easy it is to be swayed by those images if one does not have a clear image of himself. And so I think that we have to start with two fundamental questions, which are, "What is the image that I have *of* myself?" and "What is the image I have *for* myself?" The answers to those questions will shift over time, obviously. But that being said, you must know and have thought about the answers to those questions in advance.

There is an old adage, "It's not what people call you; it's what you answer to." I find myself consistently saying that to young black men and, in fact, it is something that I would say to *any* young man. It's not what people *call* you; it's what you *answer* to. When you have an assured self-image or, to put it another way, when you have a self-assured image of yourself, then you can answer to those things you want to answer to and turn a deaf ear and a blind eye to those things that you do not find appealing. I must honestly say that for all the travail and trouble and difficulty that

I've had–not unlike everybody else–that I've been clear since the age of 13 about the image *of* myself and the image I wanted *for* myself. As you read in the book, I endured a terrible beating at that age that nearly destroyed me until the words and wisdom of Dr. Martin Luther King brought me back to life, so to speak. Since that time, I've been clear about *who* I am and *who* I want to be, *what* I am and *what* I want to be.

On this point, I think there's a critical distinction to be made between what I call the "who" question and the "what" question. The media portrays images all the time that we buy into and which, for the most part, play around the edges of the "what" question. That is to say, "What do I want to be when I'm grown?" or "What should I be when I'm grown?" We get titillated by the "what" question, never, quite frankly, turning the corner to the more important question, which is the "who" question. I say to adults all the time, we have got to stop asking young black men–as we do in that cute little voice: "What do you want to be when you grow up?" That's not the question. The question is not *what* you want to be when you grow up, but *who* you want to be when you grow up. The "what" question is external and surface and *prima facie*. The "who" question is internal, more soulful and, quite frankly, more significant.

KHJ: *You've given me the perfect segue to my next question. In your book, you talked about hearing yourself on a taped playback getting after one of the producers in your studio. It was a big lesson for you in "who" you wanted to be. For the benefit of our readers, perhaps you could give the 30-second rundown of what happened that day that led you to a life-changing decision.*

Tavis: On the radio program that morning, we had a technical meltdown. There were things about the show that day that were unacceptable to me. I am a perfectionist. While I don't believe that anything's ever perfect, I believe that we can be *complete* in our work, and the show was not as complete as it could have been that day. I turned off my microphone and took the producer into a private studio. I had enough respect for her that I would never have reprimanded her in front of other people, so we went somewhere private. But then, I unloaded on her. Like I said, I turned my microphone off. But the engineers who sit in the booth are actually in control of the microphones, and there was a particular engineer in the booth that day who wasn't fond of me, apparently. This engineer turned on the microphone in the studio where I was getting after this producer and recorded everything I said onto a CD. The engineer then proceeded to make copies of that CD and distribute the copies.

Needless to say, it was an utter embarrassment for me; one, because I didn't ever mean for what I said to be made public and two, while I had the right to be upset with her, when I heard myself on the CD, I realized that I had crossed the line. It brought home a very important lesson shared with me by my dear friend and mentor Dr. Cornel West,* who said that even when we're justified, we must be dignified. I share that with people everywhere I go: Even when you're *justified*, you must always be *dignified*. What happens oftentimes is that we get dismissed because our approach is not dignified. Rightly or wrongly, the reality is that even if we are justified in our feelings, how we express them and how we display them make an enormous difference in terms of our being *heard*.

KHJ: *I think that finding a way to express frustration or anger without aggression is something a lot of men struggle with.*

Tavis: Oh, no question.

KHJ: *I mentioned earlier that your encounter with the producer led you to what I would characterize as a life-changing decision. On page 249, you write: "Faced with the CD, I couldn't deny the ugliness of my tone and the crudeness of my language. I decided not only to apologize but to stop cursing entirely, in any context . . . ." This, in my mind, is an incredibly heroic decision and one I don't think many people make—especially if they are in the habit of using profanity as an adult. So, I guess my first question is to ask you how it's going.*

Tavis: Very well! Remarkably well, in fact. First of all, anyone who knows me knows that I am a very self-assured person and so, when I decide that I am going to do something, I make it happen. That's number one. Beyond that, though, this kind of change is not something that you can succeed at without a lot of prayer. So, there has been a lot of prayer and supplication on my part because there are days when I am tempted to break my commitment.

Also, I can tell you that, for me, nothing succeeds like embarrassment. When I am embarrassed—particularly when *I* embarrass *myself* or when I

---

*Dr. Cornel West is a renowned author and professor of religion and African-American studies at Princeton University.

feel like I'm acting in a way that is beneath me, then I can turn the situation around pretty quickly. It's been a struggle all the way through, there's no question about it. But it's been more than a few years now that I've kept my commitment.

KHJ: *Sometimes when we take a U-turn like that in life, there are things we expect we will learn and then there are the lessons that come out of left field where we say, "Wow, I never saw that one coming!"*

Tavis: The one that came out of left field was how much more effectively I can get my point across without using that language–without cussing at someone. You start here–cussing to get your point across. Then you step down to screaming and yelling, but not cussing. Then you step down a bit further to just the right amount of silence. I am amazed at how my point gets across sometimes, not just without the cussing, but without having to say anything. Or, if I say anything at all, by simply telling someone, "You know what? This profoundly disappoints me. I expected better of you on this." You'd be amazed at how much more of an impact that has. We think shouting and cursing is going to get our point across. But, I found that when I stopped cussing, my points came across just as powerfully–if not more so.

The people who work for me are very loyal to me. They know that my work is born of my love for and my willingness to serve black people. They know that this, for me, is not a job. Anyone who works in this building knows it's not a job–this is our calling, this is our vocation. And so when I say to them that where my calling is concerned, where my vocation is concerned, you are here to help me and you profoundly disappointed me or you let me down–without a curse word ever being said, I've been amazed at how powerful that is.

KHJ: *And if a young man were considering following your example, what would you say is the real value of that life choice?*

Tavis: The short answer is this: I feel better about myself. I could be more profound about it, but there's no need to be. I feel better about myself and about the way I engage people.

I'll give you a quick anecdote. I was out to dinner last night with Dr. West– he was out here in L.A. for a project he was working on–and there was a table full of about eight white people adjacent to us in this restaurant. We had said absolutely nothing. We walked in, sat down and minded our own business and that was that. When they got up to leave, all eight of them came from their table to ours and introduced themselves to us. It turned out that they were big fans of mine. Having folks introduce themselves to me happens pretty regularly. But I relate this particular story because in this instance, they had not given any indication during dinner that they had any idea who I was. They had said nothing to me and I had said nothing to them. When they came over, they said, "We didn't want to interrupt you during your dinner and, quite frankly, we wanted to apologize." When I asked them why, they answered, "Because we were eavesdropping on the powerful conversation you and Dr. West were having."

I thought about that later and I realized that if I'd been there using a bunch of foul language, that may very well have turned them off. They might have said, "Oh my God, we didn't expect that out of Tavis' mouth!" And there was a time when they would have heard a lot of foul language coming out of my mouth. I don't live my life to please other people, but at the same time, there's no point in offending people. Just yesterday, I was working out with my trainer. We were outside and he had me running up and down this hill. There were some other people who were working out and, when they heard my voice, they came over and said, "You're Tavis Smiley!" It turned out that this was a couple who did not have a television, who did not believe in watching television. But they listened to my radio show every day. They said, "We heard your voice and we knew it had to be you."

The point I'm trying to make is that you just never know who is listening, and the words and language you use tell people something about you. I feel better about myself knowing that when I am talking–and when I'm going about my everyday life–what people hear is a true reflection of who I am.

KHJ: *And that takes us back to where we started–the critical "who" question! And because you've made this decision and stuck to it, you don't ever have to look over your shoulder and wonder if you have offended someone or given them a false impression of "who" you are.*

Tavis: That's right. And it doesn't matter whether you and that person ever engage or not.

KHJ: *Final question. Which living celebrity do you look to as a role model?*

Tavis: Nelson Mandela, without question. His courage, his conviction and his commitment are unique in the world.

KHJ: *Agreed! Okay, last thing—a little word association.*

Tavis: Go ahead.

KHJ: *Compassion.*

Tavis: My grandmother, who we called "Big Mama."

KHJ: *Boys don't cry.*

Tavis: False!

KHJ: *Bullies.*

Tavis: Ralph—the story in my book about the boy who beat me up every day.

KHJ: *Respect for women.*

Tavis: Cornel West. I've learned more about that from him than anyone. I grew up in a home with eight boys and two girls. There was a lot of testosterone in that house and there really wasn't a lot of conversation about those things. So having the opportunity to watch someone just a little older than me, from the old school, opening doors and pulling out chairs was a big help to me in that respect. Dr. West is kind to everyone— he's just the kindest cat in the world. I've learned more from him than just about anyone else.

Professor Roger A. Schmitz, Ph.D.

Professor Roger A. Schmitz, Ph.D.

Photo credit: Schmitz family

Roger Schmitz is an award-winning chemical engineer, a former university dean and, notably, the former vice president and associate provost of the University of Notre Dame. He is also one of the smartest and most genuine people you'll ever have the pleasure of meeting.

He joined the Notre Dame faculty in 1979 as chairman of the Department of Chemical Engineering. He went on to hold positions as the McCloskey Dean of Engineering and then special assistant to the provost, before becoming vice president and associate provost in 1987. He has been the recipient of numerous awards including a Guggenheim Fellowship, the R.H. Wilhelm Award of the American Institute of Chemical Engineers, the George Westinghouse Award of the American Society of Engineering Education, and the Allan P. Colburn Award of the American Institute of Chemical Engineers. He was awarded the Outstanding Faculty Member Award from the Notre Dame Minority Engineering Program and the Outstanding Teacher of the Year Award by the College of Engineering, University of Notre Dame. He was elected to the National Academy of Engineers in 1984.

He retired as vice president and associate provost in 1995, to return to teaching and research. He currently serves as Keating-Crawford Professor Emeritus in the university's Department of Chemical and Biomolecular Engineering.

Editor's Note

I met Roger Schmitz my freshman year of college when he was the dean of the College of Engineering at the University of Notre Dame. I wish I could tell you I was smart enough to have been a student of his (a notion so absurd it makes me laugh even today). In fact, I simply had the good luck of being friends with his daughter, who lived a few doors down from me in my dorm.

Oddly enough, there were very few drawbacks to having your best friend's father on campus. Mostly we were obliged to be slightly better behaved than we otherwise might have been (something that was, no doubt, a good thing in the long run). But this was a small price to pay for home-cooked meals and occasional access to some of the best seats in Notre Dame's stadium.

It probably goes without saying that Professor Schmitz is a man of extraordinary intelligence; but I'm going to say it anyway: He is categorically and without question one of the most brilliant people I have ever known. He is also one of the most humble, a trait which endears him to students and faculty alike.

I'm delighted to introduce the man who helped keep me out of trouble long enough to get my diploma: Notre Dame's former vice president and associate provost, Professor Roger A. Schmitz.

On a Positive Note

A few years ago when I was mulling over possible subjects for a speech I was to give to a group of students at the University of Notre Dame, I recalled a talk given by an elderly professor some 50 years earlier. I was in an audience of undergraduate students at the University of Illinois at the time, listening as he spoke about his lifetime experiences. His message made a lasting impression.

The old professor had focused on the many positive developments that had taken place over the years, claiming proudly that there had been more accomplished to benefit humankind through that period than in all previous years combined. He spoke to us about the widespread use of electricity, automobiles, airplanes, telephones, radios, television, vaccines, penicillin and so on. He pointed out that a Russian satellite, Sputnik, was orbiting the earth as he spoke, and that the university now had a digital computer. He seemed a bit astonished by it all—while, at the same time, pleased and humbled by his opportunities to contribute to such incredible progress. I recall wondering if there could possibly be anything left for my classmates and me to accomplish in our lifetimes! His generation had placed us in a privileged position, I felt.

What the old professor did not mention, however, were the era's many hardships and obstacles—challenges that made the accomplishments he had spoken of even more remarkable. For example, when he was young, books and other educational materials, even schools in some cases, were not always accessible. Travel beyond a few miles from home was practically impossible for most people. The old professor had lived through the influenza pandemic of the early 1900s and various diseases, such as cholera, diphtheria, small pox and polio, which were constant threats to health and life. Two world wars and the Korean War had been fought, two atomic bombs had been dropped, the country had been through the Great Depression in the 1930s, and the Cold War with the Soviet Union was in full swing. It was generally known that he personally did not grow up in wealth and privilege. Yet the old professor had defied the odds and worked his way successfully through all of that. It would be years before I understood that his speech had provided the roadmap showing us how to do the same.

Fifty years later, it was my turn to step into the old professor's shoes. Translating the gist of his message to cover five decades of my experiences, I spoke to my students about extensive space explorations, advances in medicine and health care, the end of the Cold War and the Iron Curtain, and the passage of civil rights legislation. I hardly needed to point out that advances in electronic technologies had led to a plethora of conveniences and devices, including personal computers, wireless telephones, worldwide communication, cell phones and the Internet.

There were dark times during those years, of course. My 50 years also had witnessed assassinations and a nuclear arms race, wars in Vietnam, Iraq and other parts of the world, civil unrest and the riots of the 1960s, scandals in government, increased use of illegal drugs, and a general erosion of family values. When I spoke to my students, however, I followed the old professor's lead and focused my speech on the positives. I did so because I have lived long enough to finally learn what my old professor had known all along—*that those individuals who experience the greatest personal success and who play a significant part in advancing the well being of the world do so by consistently seizing opportunities and taking advantage of what is going right in their time, and refusing to be limited by whatever is going wrong.* I hoped to pass this lesson along to my students by pointing out to them the many possibilities for success that lay before them—possibilities well beyond anything the old professor and my group of classmates could have imagined 50 years ago.

As it has been for every generation, the world in which my students and you are living is a mixed bag of opportunities and obstacles. Noticeably, from my perspective, the pace of change is faster than ever. It directly affects your generation more than ever, positively and negatively. You are bombarded nonstop with activities, objects, and devices of all sorts. This plethora makes lives interesting and exciting, but also complicated, increasingly stressful, over-scheduled and excessively busy—*CrazyBusy*, as Edward Hallowell puts it in the title of his recent book.* So fast is the change that it often *outpaces* one's ability to adjust, to evaluate consequences, and to sort out good information from bad. Television

---

*Edward M. Hallowell, M.D., *CrazyBusy: Overstretched, Overbooked, and About to Snap!* (New York: Ballantine Books, 2006).

programs, movies, personal computers, the Internet, communications systems, and so on all have marvelous benefits to offer, but they're not always in tune with your best interests. Neither are certain societal trends, such as the erosion of moral standards and family values. Sometimes we old-timers call it a mess. But like it or not, it is the reality of your life and you can't escape it.

However you may view the starting point, I'm sure that each of you hopes to go on to lead a fulfilling and successful life in the end. One predictor of your ultimate success lies in your ability to view today's picture as one of unusual privilege and opportunity. By this I do not mean that you should ignore problems that exist in the world. Far from it. There are difficult moral and ethical question that you will have to face. But, like the men and women of previous generations, you must find a path through these complexities. You will need the strength of character to maintain a positive mental attitude regardless of what life throws your way, the good judgment to take advantage of opportunities, the self-discipline to rise above the negatives, and the courage to focus on what is good and humanly decent. These basics that define fulfilling and successful lives do not change, though they may be more difficult to discern in this *CrazyBusy* world. So choose your paths wisely. Hold fast to all that is good. This is your *life!* Live it well.

Kevin Willis

Kevin Willis

Photo credit: NBA photos

A seven-foot tall, 23-year veteran of the NBA, Kevin Willis is a force to be reckoned with.

He was Atlanta's first-round draft pick in the 1984 NBA draft and the 11th pick overall in the league. For the 10 years that followed, Kevin and teammates Dominique Wilkins, Spud Webb, Doc Rivers, and Moses Malone proved a potent and winning combination for the Hawks, leading the team to seven play-off appearances. Following a break-out season in 1992, Kevin was named to the NBA and Eastern Conference All-Star teams. In 1994, he left the Hawks and over the course of the next decade brought his dominating presence as both a center and power forward to the Miami Heat, the Golden State Warriors, the Denver Nuggets, the Toronto Raptors and the San Antonio Spurs. He was an integral member of the Spurs 2003 NBA Championship team and is one of only 15 players in NBA history with over 16,000 career points and 11,000 career rebounds.

Kevin returned to Atlanta in 2004, where he played for another two years. In 2007, he was tapped by the Dallas Mavericks to help them in their bid for the NBA Championship. Over the course of his 23 years in the NBA, he cemented his reputation as a player who was tough on the court and a leader in the locker room. True to form, Kevin went to Dallas not just to help the *team,* but to offer guidance and support to the *players.* And he did so gladly, knowing full well that most of his work would take place behind the scenes rather than in front of the cameras.

During his time with the Mavericks, Kevin held the distinction of being the oldest active player in the NBA and he became the second oldest active player in NBA history. In his second appearance with the Mavericks, he became the oldest player ever to score in an NBA game.

Off the court, Kevin devotes his time to Willis & Walker, a high-end specialty clothing line he founded in 1988 with his former Michigan State Spartans teammate Ralph Walker.

Editor's Note

The first word most people use to describe Kevin Willis is tall. At seven feet, this is perhaps no surprise. But I've had the pleasure of knowing Kevin for a few years now and if I were asked to describe him, the adjective "tall" wouldn't even make the top 10. Instead I would choose words like talented, precise, driven, disciplined, soft-spoken, generous and kind.

I met Kevin for the first time at a charity golf tournament in Atlanta. He was one of the guest celebrity players and I was one of many volunteers. Despite my decided lack of status at this event, he took time to talk to me. He asked me what I did for a living and seemed genuinely interested in my answer. When I mentioned this book, he accepted my invitation to be a part of it on the spot. It was evident that he had something he wanted to say, and not just as a professional basketball player, but as a man and a father.

We met at the Atlanta office of Willis & Walker, where we talked for over an hour. His answers to my questions were honest, direct and personal. No topic was off-limits and nothing was sugar-coated. He told the truth as he knows it–as he lives it.

I am honored to introduce the very smart and very talented, Mr. Kevin Willis.

A Conversation with Kevin Willis

KHJ: *I know you have strong feelings about violence and the way in which it permeates our culture, especially popular culture.*

Kevin: Yeah, I do.

KHJ: *Tell me about that, if you would.*

Kevin: Frankly, I'm just tired of it. I'm sick and tired of all of the shooting and the killing in video games and movies and whatever other media is coming down the pike. I'm not talking about bang-bang cartoon violence. I'm talking about serious graphics that depict people being maimed, killed and murdered. We get enough of that in everyday life. And when you're in middle school or high school and you see this kind of violence over and over—whether it's on the news or in your neighborhood—and then you have it reinforced in videos and movies, what you take away from it, I believe, is, "This is okay. I'm used to this. This is what I want to do one day." You start to think that this kind of violence is not that bad. Most kids don't think it's a big deal and they'll tell you it doesn't affect them. But how many times now have you seen kids going into their high schools or the mall and shooting people? I *know* that some of this, not all of it, but some of it comes from these video games and movies and all the rest. I monitor my own son and I put certain restrictions on what he can see, whether it's MTV or reality shows or video games. I just don't allow him access to what I consider garbage. But for the other young men out there, all I can do is to try and state my case and make them aware of the fact that it can (and does) affect them.

KHJ: *I'd like to dig a little deeper into this if I could.*

Kevin: Sure.

KHJ: *When I met with Dominique [Wilkins], he talked about how to deal with violence, particularly the kind of mean-spirited bullying that goes on in middle school and high school. One thing he said that really* struck me was this—and I think he is absolutely correct—that bullying and violence are rooted in fear.

Kevin: Oh, no doubt!

KHJ: *Taking that as our starting point, I want to ask you about a very particular area where bullying and outright violence are serious problems. To do that, I need to begin by laying some groundwork. I read recently that, for the last decade or so, the vast majority of hate crimes reported to police are based on perceived sexual orientation. And while I don't have any statistics to back this up, I'd be willing to bet that being a gay man in middle school or high school is a hell of a challenge. The reason I bring this up with you is this. You are a professional athlete—the pinnacle of masculinity—and yet you also work in the world of fashion where, I imagine, you have to interact with people of different sexual orientations. So, my question is, what has that been like? How have you come to terms with it, and what advice do you have to offer?*

Kevin: Well, first of all, I don't want to sit here and lie to you and tell you that I'm perfectly comfortable with homosexuality. I think I am like a lot of straight men in that respect. However—and this is an important *however*—I try very hard not to pass judgment. None of us is in a position to sit in judgment of another human being. As an African-American I know what it feels like to bear someone's intolerance and prejudice, so I do not want to be a party to that. When I read about some guys beating on someone just because he's gay . . . well, I think it is just about the worst thing they can do. We can disagree with someone's choices. We can be honest in saying that it makes us uncomfortable or whatever, but we don't *ever* have the right to be violent. You don't get to express your discomfort with someone's sexuality through violence or through words that degrade, just like you don't get to do that based on someone's color or religion or ethnicity. If you're feeling like you want to hurt someone just because they're gay, I've got news for you: *It has nothing to do with them!* All that hate, all that anger—it's about your own insecurities and your own manhood feeling threatened. So, am I 100-percent comfortable with homosexuality? No. But do I feel threatened by it? No. Why? Because I am secure in my manhood.

KHJ: *Do you feel as though this is something that you continue to work on?*

Kevin: Yes, at times. I actually caught myself recently. I saw two guys in the mall who were obviously gay and being affectionate with each other. They weren't making out or being inappropriate in that way, but just showing their affection. I stopped in my tracks and I found myself staring at them, judging them harshly, thinking, "How in the *world* can they do that? How can they feel that way?" But afterwards, when I got back home, I felt very badly about what I had done. I told myself, "That's their preference and that's their business, and that's just me judging." I chastised *myself* and put *myself* back in check. I had no right to do what I did. They didn't touch me. They didn't say anything to me. They didn't affect me in any way other than by showing their affection for each other the same way many hetero couples do. It may make me uncomfortable and I may struggle with my feelings about it, but I have no right to be so judgmental, and I checked myself for that.

KHJ: *So what is it that young men can take away from your experience?*

Kevin: Live and let live. That is what is right and it is what is required of you. Live and let live and keep yourself in check. And when you *can't* do that, you need to sit down and ask yourself why not. Why can't I let that person be who he is? Why does that threaten me? Then put your energy into working on *yourself* and leave whoever it is alone!

KHJ: *What was one of the defining moments for you in your life in terms of moving from boy to man?*

Kevin: I grew up in Detroit–a tough area in Detroit. Our neighborhood started out as a nice area but turned tough and crazy. There were a hundred ways to go down the wrong path there. I thank God I had parents who truly gave me the tools I needed to adapt to that life without becoming consumed by it. They taught me to keep the focus on family, keep the focus on God, and keep the focus on what is important. I kept those values dear and close to my heart, knowing full well that things were not always going to be sweet.

KHJ: *Can you tell me what you did specifically?*

Kevin: First of all, I made a promise to myself that I would never do anything that would get me too far off track, whether it was being a follower or whether it was being a guy who felt peer pressure to do what everybody else was doing. I never fell into any of that junk. I never fell into drinking, never smoked, never did drugs. I stayed away because I loved my parents and didn't want to do anything that might hurt them. I did some crazy things and got in trouble like all kids do. But I never did the kinds of things that can tear a family apart.

The second thing I did was, when I got to high school I decided that, no matter what, I was going to graduate. Graduating wasn't a given in my neighborhood. So I did everything that I thought I could do to graduate. I didn't do it right all the time, but I made certain that, come June 20, I was walking across that stage to get my diploma!

KHJ: *How about lessons you learned playing basketball?*

Kevin: There are so many . . . I remember the first time I tried out for a basketball team I was in the ninth grade. I was six feet or six-one, but I'd never played basketball before, so I didn't make the team. We moved to a new school the next year and the basketball coach, Billy Carter, saw me walking through the hallways. He asked me if I played basketball. I was still feeling badly about not making the team at my last school, so I told him no, I didn't play. He said to me, "Well, do you *want* to play basketball?" And I said, "Nope!" But he kept on me, and I finally agreed to tryout. He took me into the gym and very casually, he said, "Let me see you dunk." By now I'm standing at least six feet three inches but, truth be told, I couldn't dunk the basketball! Wouldn't you know, the gym was packed that day, and so even though I was afraid, I knew I *had* to dunk that ball because there were too many people watching for me not to!

So, here it is, my first time ever trying to dunk: I get the ball, I run up, I jump with everything I've got . . . and I *miss*. I literally fell on the floor. I got up, took the ball down, went up toward the basket and . . . I fall *again*. *But*, that second time, I could feel that I'd come close. So I went up again, and on the *third* try, I dunked it. I was so amazed–I couldn't believe it! I wanted to jump for joy but, of course I had to play it cool!

It was something I'll never forget, and I walked off the court that day knowing two things: one, that I was going to do everything I could to be the best basketball player I could be, and two, that I would never quit trying to achieve a goal that I set for myself–not goals that others may have set *for* me, but goals I set for myself. It's been 27 years since that day in the gym and I've never taken on anything that I've quit. I can't remember any time in my life when I've taken on something and things got so tough that I just said, "Forget it."

KHJ: *What about people who might say, "Well, that's easy for him because he was good enough at basketball to play professionally and I am just a normal guy"?*

Kevin: Well, first of all I would tell them that playing pro ball is about a lot more than just having the talent. It takes equal amounts talent, hard work, determination and sacrifice. Second, *every* person is blessed with some kind of gift–I don't care who you are. Everybody has some unique ability or insight or passion that they have been blessed with.

I believe that we are meant to take the gifts we are given and turn them into something in our lives. With basketball, I felt like God had given me a gift, a tool. And I believe he was telling me, "Okay, I'm gonna give this to you and I'm gonna see if you can take it and shape it and make it into something that is unbelievable." And I took that gift with faith, and with the support of family and a few very good friends, and I made it happen. But in truth, every person has the right and the duty to look at the gifts he or she has been given and make the most of them.

KHJ: *Who is your hero?*

Kevin: My brother. I've patterned my life after him. He played ball for a little while–he was good, too–but he decided it wasn't for him. Instead, he went to work to help support the family. He got married out of high school and became a police officer. I always admired the fact that he never got into drinking or smoking or any of that craziness. He stayed away from trouble and was always mature–too mature for his time maybe! He had a gift, whether he knew it or not, of strength of character. His life set a good example for me and others of what it took to grow up and make something of yourself in a very tough environment. He set that example each day as he went about his business as a brother, then a husband and father, and as a member of the community.

My high school coach also is one of my heroes. He had a gift for reaching out to young men and letting them see that they could accomplish more than they thought they could. Without his faith in me, who knows where I would be today.

KHJ: *What is some of the best advice you received when you were young?*

Kevin: The best advice I would say was from my father. He always told me, "Son, never be a follower. Be a leader, always." He taught me that the best people in this world are the ones who remain humble and who stay true to what they believe in their hearts. He often tells me now that I am one of the top five men he knows in terms of heart, kindness and character. I cannot tell you what that means to me.

KHJ: *When you say "character," what does that mean to you exactly?*

Kevin: Good question. When I think about character, it's hard to say right off the bat *exactly* what it is. I do know that your character is what gets you through life. And I know that if you don't have character, you're going to be lost because you'll have nothing to gravitate to, or to hold on to, in the hard times. Character defines what you stand for, what and who are important to you, and how you deal with people. In my experience, if you have character, you gain the respect of the people around you, and you give them respect as well. That's key.

I'll give you an example–and it's one that I use a lot. Josh Smith is a new, young player with the Atlanta Hawks. I've been playing professionally for 20 years, so when I started playing, he wasn't even born! But he's a person, he's my teammate, he's a young man–that's enough for me. That warrants respect right there. I respect Josh just like I respect someone who's older than I am or someone my age. And I appreciate the respect he gives me. It's a give and take. Now, that doesn't mean I don't have things to teach him. I've been around a long time and I can tell him what's right and what's wrong, what is going to work and what's not. But I do it man to man. I begin with respect. I offer my respect to everyone I meet until they give me a reason to do otherwise. That's how I operate.

KHJ: *If you could go back in time and talk with your 15-year-old self, what would you say to that young man?*

Kevin: I would say to be a little bit more attentive to the needs of others. People try to tell you that tending to emotional needs isn't masculine or whatever. Well, I'm a man and I have a sensitive side to me–just like *every* other guy I know. And so when someone is really attentive to me, I appreciate it. It makes me feel good. It makes me feel like, "Man, I needed that!"

KHJ: *Do you think you are alone in feeling that way?*

Kevin: No way. But guys get caught up in that trap of "big boys don't cry," and that's so ridiculous. It's basically telling you to ignore your feelings. But if you ignore your emotions, they're going to find a way out whether it's through something appropriate, like talking with a friend or punching a bag, or through something inappropriate, like punching some*one*. I was asked a question two weeks ago, "When was the last time you cried?" I said, "Last week!" I was listening to this music and it sort of took me somewhere and it made me feel good. I cried tears of joy at being truly appreciative and truly grateful for where I'm at.

KHJ: *I want to end with a short word association on three items. Normally it's four, but you just addressed the first one, which is "Boys don't cry." So we'll begin with the second.*

Kevin: Sure, go ahead.

KHJ: *Respect for women.*

Kevin: Respect is the ultimate thing you can give a woman; everything else follows from that: love, appreciation, understanding, relationship. It's all rooted in there.

KHJ: *Compassion.*

Kevin: Without it you have no heart. You have no connection to people, no understanding, no care, no love . . . you don't have much of anything.

KHJ: *Bullies.*

Kevin: [They] need to stay home. Bullies act from insecurity and self-doubt, and their behavior is inexcusable, period.

Captain Howard "Rusty" Petrea, USN (Ret.)

Captain Howard "Rusty" Petrea, USN (Ret.)

Photo credit: Petrea family

Capt. Howard "Rusty" Petrea is a former naval officer and pilot who retired to North Carolina with the intention of fulfilling a lifelong dream of building his own private golf course. That dream changed, however, when his wife, Carol, pointed out to him the vast number of underserved and at-risk youth in and around the county where they lived. In response, Rusty put his dream on permanent hold, choosing instead to dedicate his time and resources to serving those children and their families through the creation of The First Tee of Brunswick County, a local chapter of the national First Tee organization founded by Tiger Woods' father, Earl Woods, and former Pres. George Herbert Walker Bush. Under Rusty and Carol's leadership, The First Tee of Brunswick County quickly became one of the fastest growing and most successful chapters in the organization's history.

Before devoting his time, energy and personal resources to The First Tee, Rusty spent 27 years in the Navy, retiring with the rank of captain. His military years were highlighted by senior leadership positions, such as command of a strike-fighter squadron and, during Operation Desert Storm, command of a carrier air wing. He also led units in Somalia and Bosnia. In his last active duty assignment, he was a senior adviser to the commander in chief U.S. Pacific, traveling extensively throughout the Asia-Pacific. He was directly involved with Europe and the Balkans as executive assistant to Adm. Leighton W. Smith, Jr.,* who was commander of NATO Implementation Forces in Bosnia, commander in chief of Allied Forces Southern Europe, and commander in chief of U.S. Naval Forces Europe.

In addition to his work with The First Tee, Rusty serves as chief operating officer of Global Perspectives Inc., a leadership development consulting company.

---

*See Admiral Smith's essay on page 11.

Editor's Note

I love telling this story about Rusty because, more than anything else I could say about him—about how hard-working, uncomplaining and downright extraordinary he is—this story, I think, captures him best.

I had traveled to meet him at the site of The First Tee program that he and his wife had founded in Brunswick County, North Carolina. I knew he was a retired naval officer and that he had put aside his lifelong dream of building his own personal golf course in order to create a golf program for underprivileged kids. But beyond that, I didn't know what to expect. I drove out to the site one sweltering afternoon, making my way along a dusty road bordered on either side by dense North Carolina underbrush, until finally I turned a corner to find myself facing the lush green of a golf course.

There were several buildings straight ahead that housed golfing supplies, maintenance equipment and an office. I imagined Rusty was in there somewhere conducting business or making calls to potentials donors and volunteers—anything that involved air-conditioning, I hoped! I got out of my car and poked around, but there was no sign of him. The only person I could find was some poor maintenance guy out on the fairway, soaked through with sweat from laboring in the August heat. I headed over to ask him if he knew where Rusty might be. As soon as he saw me coming, he stopped what he was doing, took off his gloves and walked to me with his hand outstretched. "Rusty Petrea," he said introducing himself, "Nice to see you."

I'm humbled to introduce to you a man of unparalleled character and generosity, Capt. Howard "Rusty" Petrea.

Character, Integrity and Perseverance

My wife, Carol, and I both spent our professional careers in the United States Navy. When we retired, we settled in on the coast of North Carolina to pursue a lifelong dream of building our own, personal golf course! It was a big dream and, looking back at it now, a largely selfish one. Thankfully, soon after we launched full-force into this "dream project," Carol had a profound change of heart. She saw the 11,000 school-age youth in our rural county without a YMCA or Boys and Girls Club and she knew this golf course could no longer be for our personal use. Instead, Carol's vision was that our course would be for the opportunity and use of underprivileged and underserved youth in Brunswick County. The day Carol changed our mission, I started looking around for a "program fit." I quickly discovered The First Tee.

The First Tee is a national organization with over 200 local chapters nationwide. It was created in November 1997, when former President George H.W. Bush, PGA Tour Commissioner Tim Finchem, Tiger Woods' father, Earl Woods, and others gathered together in New York's Central Park and announced that it was the last day that golf would be a sport only for the elite. Our Chapter, The First Tee of Brunswick County, and our facility–the golf course we built not for ourselves, but exclusively for The First Tee kids–is The Golf Club at Cinghiale Creek. Cinghiale (which means wild boar in Italian) has a learning center complete with a computer center, locker rooms, indoor putting green, and a state-of-the-art golf simulator (with Pebble Beach in the database!).

Why am I telling you this? Because The First Tee is not simply a place for kids to learn to play golf. Instead, golf is the means through which The First Tee teaches and promotes character development; and it does so as well as or better than any program I've encountered. It is founded on nine core values. These nine core values are interrelated, and together they are qualities shared by every great leader and by all persons of character: honesty, integrity, perseverance, confidence, judgment, responsibility, sportsmanship, courtesy and respect.

The youth who participate in The First Tee typically come from difficult economic situations. Life is hard for them, and it is hard in ways that most children, thankfully, don't ever have to experience. Yet, each week, they do whatever it takes to get here. Sometimes the challenges our kids are facing go well beyond economic. Take Andrew,* for example, who first came to The First Tee back in 2005. He was only 14 years old at the time, but he had seen and experienced the pain and disappointment of someone three times his age. Andrew had been diagnosed with brain cancer when he was just two years old; he then spent the next two years in and out of hospitals as doctors worked to save his life. He endured multiple painful surgeries along with several rounds of chemotherapy until, finally, the cancer went into remission.

One side effect of Andrew's chemotherapy was that it temporarily accelerated his body's growth. An avid sports fan and highly competitive by nature, Andrew was able to compete and, in fact, excel in every sport he tried. But his growth spurt came to an abrupt end as the trauma to his brain began to take its toll. As time went by and his friends continued to grow bigger and stronger, Andrew discovered he could no longer remain competitive.

By age 10, his body was stunted and his joints were riddled with pain from the chemotherapy. His head, which was slightly too large for his body—another side effect of the treatment—was covered in scars; and as he approached middle school, teasing and name-calling became the order of the day. Life was miserable for him. Still, he forged ahead as best he could, looking for the positive in even the bleakest situation. (His parents told me stories of Andrew coming from school and joyously telling them, "I wasn't the slowest at school today. I beat one other kid!") But by age 13, he had had enough of the failure and the mistreatment. So when his parents told him about The First Tee, not surprisingly, he had zero interest in coming. To Andrew, The First Tee simply represented another place to feel different—another place to come in last. However, at his core he is a person of tremendous courage, and ultimately his courage got the better of him.

It wasn't easy for him. It wasn't easy to get to The First Tee facility each week; it wasn't easy to be the new guy, especially when you're a little bit different; it wasn't easy to try again—to risk failure and disappointment again—but he *did*! He worked at his game and he worked his way through

---

*Not his real name.

the core values. He made mistakes along the way, as everyone does, but he kept moving forward. In time, he became a competitive golfer and, more importantly, a tremendous person. Today, at age 16, he is one of The First Tee's shining stars.

But this is real life and so the story does not have a magical ending. Andrew didn't grow 10 inches and the pain in his joints has not subsided. He has not been cured of his cancer; instead he still has to make an annual trek to the doctor for an MRI to see whether it has re-emerged. Yet, even as I write this, he continues to be a model of courage and persistence in the face of these overwhelming obstacles.

I tell you Andrew's story in the hope that you will take away two things. First is the understanding that nothing will make you a better man faster than having to face a seemingly insurmountable challenge. They say that what doesn't kill you makes you stronger. I say that what doesn't kill you *can* make you stronger; but only if you let it make you stronger. It is a choice. After all, how many people do you know who have allowed the hardships they've faced to make them bitter or angry?

Second, I want you to understand that character develops over time. It is an ongoing process that takes years and requires practice, demonstration, improvement and accountability. Do not be discouraged when you fall short! Everyone does—many times. Simply pick yourself up and start again. Just keep moving forward and you will eventually arrive at the place in life where you want to be.

I will close with a challenge. I challenge you to choose one of the nine core values and incorporate it into your life. Take the core value of honesty, for example. See if you can go one entire month without telling a single lie (or half-truth, exaggeration, or lie of omission). I promise you it will be a *lot* tougher than you can imagine. But it will also be an invaluable, eye-opening life lesson—one that is *impossible* to duplicate simply by thinking, writing or talking about honesty! Nothing takes the place of *doing*. If you can find it in yourself to make it through one month, then try to make it for two months. Fairly quickly, you will become known as someone who can always be trusted to tell the truth. How many people in your life can you say that about?

When you have gained some mastery over honesty, then review the list of core values and select another—courtesy, sportsmanship, perseverance or confidence—and work to incorporate it into your life as well. Expect ups and downs. Know that at times you will fail. But if you can continue to work towards these nine core values, I guarantee you will succeed.

I am sometimes asked whether I ever have a tinge of regret at having given up my dream of owning my own golf course. I can tell you with absolute honesty (core value #1!) that I have never once regretted my decision. In fact, when I think of that dream now, I can only see how shallow and empty my life would have been. It was a selfish dream and I am relieved that my wife had the wisdom to see that. Sometimes I think of myself rambling around on that course all alone, and then I look around at all the kids and volunteers here at The First Tee of Brunswick County, and I am so deeply grateful. The difference it has made in my life . . . well, there simply are no words to describe it. There's just no comparison; in fact, it isn't even close.

The Nine Core Values of The First Tee

These nine core values are only words unless you incorporate them into your life, and that is no easy task. Here is how I would describe each of them:

- Honesty: That means in all things, from being truthful with others to being honest with yourself.
- Integrity: It is closely tied to honesty and requires you to do the right thing, even when no one is watching.
- Perseverance: You persist towards your goal, even when the going gets tough and you want to quit. Andrew, whose story I related to you, is a model of perseverance.
- Confidence: And I don't mean cocky. Be confident in the things you do, the choices you make and in yourself, no matter what the obstacles.
- Judgment: That pesky inner voice that tells you when you are not making a good choice. Each time you use good judgment, it is easier to do it the next time.
- Responsibility: This means being accountable both for your actions and your dealings with others. In short, can you be trusted to do the right thing—are you a dependable person in all you do?
- Sportsmanship: Play by the rules, be a good winner and acknowledge defeat gracefully. Notice I didn't say "accept defeat"

gracefully. Learn from it and put in the effort so that the next time, someone else can be a good sport in defeat. Importantly, sportsmanship applies on and off the playing field.
- Courtesy: We seem to have lost our way here, in my view. You don't have to like someone to be courteous. Courtesy is the habit of successful people, even when things don't go their way.
- Respect: Start with respecting yourself and who you are as a person. Then you can move to others and show them the respect that they are due as other human beings. This is an interesting trait–if you practice respecting yourself and others long enough, even if you start out faking it, you will find that it becomes real.

Fred K. Bruney

Fred K. Bruney

Photo credit: Philadelphia Eagles

Described as "pound for pound . . . one of the toughest football players in the nation,"* Fred Bruney's football career began at Ohio State University under the legendary Woody Hayes. Fred was twice named All-American and, upon graduation from college in 1953, he was drafted by the Cleveland Browns. Over the course of his career he would play for the San Francisco 49ers, the Pittsburgh Steelers, the Los Angeles Rams, and the Boston Patriots. A dominating defensive back, Fred was named All-Pro in 1960 and was twice selected to play in the Pro-Bowl.

He began working as a player coach with the Boston Patriots in 1962 and, in 1963, retired as a player to begin coaching full time. In addition to coaching with the New York Giants and the Indianapolis Colts, he was the defensive coordinator and assistant head coach for the Tampa Bay Buccaneers, the Atlanta Falcons, and the Philadelphia Eagles, who he helped coach to the 1981 Super Bowl.

The originator of the "safety blitz," Fred Bruney retired from coaching in 1997.

---

*Steve King, "The Championships Kept Coming," *Cleveland Browns*, (April 8, 2005), http://www.clevelandbrowns.com/article.php?id=4144, (quoting from the 1953 *Cleveland Brown's National Football League Guide*).

Editor's Note

I met former NFL player and Philadelphia Eagles coach Fred Bruney at his home in North Carolina on a beautiful summer morning about three weeks before the start of football season. I sat fascinated as he gave me an insider's view of the strategies different coaches were employing in the preseason and what he felt they were looking for from different players. It was the most insightful analysis I'd ever heard–a true coach's perspective on professional football, and very different from the analysis I was used to hearing from television announcers. "The announcers have a job to do and most of them do it pretty well," Fred said graciously. "But what someone thinks is happening can be very different from what is actually happening from the coach's point of view."

Having coached professionally for more than 35 years, Fred Bruney has had the opportunity to watch countless players come face to face with both tremendous success and terrible disappointment, and he has seen it bring out both the best and the worst in them. One of the many things of which he is certain after all this time is the fact that it is the way we choose to respond to the events in our lives–and not the events themselves–that make or break us. Fred never saw this more clearly than he did the day his friend and mentor, the legendary Woody Hayes, made a choice that would end his coaching career. It is a heartbreaking story; but Fred shares it here, along with examples from his own life, in the hope that the benefit of their experiences will allow you to see the choices you face more clearly and to make those choices well.

I'm delighted to introduce former NFL player and coach (and the originator of the safety blitz!), Mr. Fred K. Bruney.

On Choices

I was fortunate to earn a living doing what I loved to do. I played professional football in the American and National Football Leagues for eight seasons and coached professionally for 33 more. Although I wasn't the biggest or fastest defensive back in the league, I received my share of honors, including being selected to play in the Pro Bowl on two occasions. Looking back, I know all too well now how fortunate I was to go to work every day and love my chosen profession. As I sit here and reminisce—now that I am retired and have time to do that—I would like for you to read this and know that I am concerned as I think of the many choices that face you as you begin making your way to manhood. It is my hope that I can provide a little insight that might help you along the way.

Your world is so much more difficult than the one I grew up in during the 1940s and 1950s. When I was young, we would play all day, come home to eat lunch or dinner, and go back out and play until our parents whistled for us to come in or the street lights came on. If we got in a fight, we used our fists—not weapons. And if we were really wild, we might try a sip of beer or a cigarette—not pills or other drugs.

Nowadays, it seems that drugs and alcohol are commonplace, a virtual rite of passage. No doubt, the temptation to try them is great. But I promise you they are not the glamorous distraction your peers would have you believe. As both a young player and a seasoned coach, I watched far too many careers destroyed by these and other temptations. It takes strength of character and tremendous self-confidence to walk away from something your friends are doing, and when we are young, most of us are simply too weak or too immature to say "no." Still, I hope you will find a way to resist. I know of no adult who looks back on alcohol or drug use from their youth and feels proud. In fact, more often than not, these episodes serve only as a source of embarrassment.

The good news is that God gives you many opportunities in life to succeed. It's up to you to look for and take advantage of those opportunities when they come. I can tell you that the best men I know are the ones who did so. Day by day, they made sound friendships, showed good judgment and just generally went out of their way to be good guys. They made good choices.

My family was from Martins Ferry, Ohio. My mother died 18 days after I was born, leaving my three-year-old brother and me with a devastated father. Those were the "depression years," and finding a job was very hard. My dad's parents offered to take me in so he could find work, an offer that he gratefully accepted. My grandparents had a large family and it was through them that I learned about sharing, honesty and tough love. My uncles all played football at the local high school, so I was exposed to that sport early on. I loved it—and found that I had a knack for it. However, I wasn't very big. (In fact, when I played in the pros, I was a lanky 185-pounder.) Although I rarely thought of my size as being detrimental, I know it made me try that much harder to excel. I was fortunate to play on an undefeated team my senior year in high school and won enough awards and acclamations to be given a football scholarship to Ohio State University, a Big Ten school.

In my sophomore year of college, I made the varsity team. The legendary Woody Hayes became my coach in my junior year. All was not rosy under Woody's demanding coaching personality. He pushed his players to do their best both on and off the field and took an interest in their personal lives. Like most good coaches, he also assumed the role of a surrogate father. I needed that on more than one occasion, as I could get a little high strung. There were times when I did things of which I wasn't too proud and boy, he'd let me have it!

I remember one of these incidents particularly well. Coach Hayes put in a special play all week in practice, with me hiding the ball on my hip after it was snapped through the quarterback's legs. This play was called the "John Pont Special" because John Pont ran the play at Miami of Ohio two times for two touchdowns when Woody was the head coach there. Near the end of the first half of a game, Coach Hayes sent in the John Pont Special with a player who had not practiced the play. I was sure my teammate had made a mistake and told him to go back to the bench. He started back and Woody motioned him to go back to the huddle. "Here he comes again," I thought. I told him "No way!" and sent him back to the bench. We ran the play . . . and I was tackled on the two yard line just as the half ended—with no time left on the clock for another play. We were all headed for the dressing room when all of a sudden I felt a hand on the neck of my jersey. I knew who it was without looking. Woody was furious and told me in the locker room that if I ever pulled a stunt like that again, he would ask for my uniform. Boy did that bring me back to reality!

I made a bad choice out on that field because of my own ego—and the entire team paid the price. Fortunately, Coach Hayes gave me a second chance. However, the time would come when he himself would not be so lucky.

There was an incident that took place long after I'd left Ohio State, when Woody hit a player on the other team as he ran out of bounds on the Ohio State sideline. Everyone who saw that game on TV knew that would be the end of Woody's coaching career at Ohio State. What few people knew, however, was that Woody at one time was a great boxer. I'm sure his hitting the opposing player was a natural reflex triggered by anger and frustration in a volatile situation. It was wrong and I won't for a moment try to defend what he did; but hitting a player just wasn't Woody. Here, though, is an example of why we must always work to make the best possible choices, *no matter* the circumstances. Regardless of what came before or what hardship we have endured, in the end, we are responsible for *each and every* choice we make. In this case, despite his achievements as the head coach of a very successful Ohio State football program, the great Woody Hayes was forced to resign.

The most jarring part of this lesson for me sprang from the fact that *Woody was a good guy*. He was a generous and caring person. For example, after I graduated from Ohio State but before I entered the pros, Woody gave me a job as the freshman football coach so I could be nearby to care for my wife when she was ill for a year. Still, his actions during those few seconds cost him the job he loved!

Despite what you may see in Hollywood or professional sports, the truth is that consequences and responsibility fall on everyone in equal measure. I loved and respected Woody until the day he died. He spoke at the Dapper Dan Sportsman of the Year banquet about me when I received an award and accompanied me when I was a coach with the Eagles to the 1981 Super Bowl. It meant so much to have him there. Years later I was thrilled to watch as he was honored by Ohio State University by "dotting the 'i.'"* It was a wonderful and emotional moment, seeing him back on the field he

---

*Being chosen to "dot the 'i'" at Ohio State is a significant honor. Woody Hayes, Bob Hope, Jack Nicklaus, and James "Buster" Douglas are among a select few non-band members who have ever been so honored. During half-time, the Ohio State band marches out and writes the word "Ohio" in script. Then, as the crowd waits in suspense to find out who has been chosen, the honoree walks out and takes his place at the top of the "i."

loved. But the lesson he taught me in his saddest hour has never left me.

Of course, having the courage to make the right choices, whether in sports or in life, can take many forms. Sometimes it means standing up to bullies; other times it might mean turning the other cheek. And sometimes, it means giving it your best when you really don't want to be there at all. My son, Chuck, was somewhat shy and a bit of a loner growing up. A change in coaching jobs once required us to move from New Jersey to Atlanta when he was 13 years old. That's a tough time to pull up roots. A lot of neighborhoods had their own swim clubs in Atlanta, and so my wife and I encouraged him to join our neighborhood team and participate in the meets. We thought it would be a good way to meet kids and strike up some friendships. Well, as often happens, the kids in the neighborhood had already formed their cliques. Being shy and new to the group, Chuck hated going to practice and used any excuse to try to avoid them. He woke up every morning saying that he was sick to his stomach, didn't want to go to practice, and constantly wanted to quit the team. I insisted he go, but very often he would come home and tell us that he was so nervous he threw up during practice. I appreciated the fact that he was trying so hard, and I told him so. But he hated going and repeatedly asked me if he could quit the team.

I finally made a deal with him. The first meet was coming up and I said that if he would give it another few days and give it his best at the meet, then, if he still didn't like being on the swim team, I would let him quit. About four days before the meet, he ran through the door yelling that Stan, the coach who had pushed him so hard to excel, had told all the kids that if they weren't throwing up and pushing themselves 100 percent like Chuck, they weren't going to win. Of course, the coach had no idea how much Chuck had been struggling with nerves and lack of confidence. And though my wife and I got quite a chuckle out of this, the recognition from Stan made all the difference in the world to Chuck. He had been singled out for his courage in sticking to it and giving it his very best under very trying circumstances. He went on to become a very competitive swimmer and then became a coach himself during college. He learned much from this experience and he continues to call upon it even as an adult when things get tough.

I hope your choices will be mostly good ones. I say "mostly" because no one gets through life without making his or her share of mistakes. When those mistakes happen, whatever you do, don't despair over your failure–learn from them and become stronger for it. And don't give up. Even at my age I can still find myself having to climb out from some hole I've dug for myself or staring at a mountain I must scale, and I can feel overwhelmed. But then I think of paraplegics who play basketball from their wheelchairs, or amputees who ski down the mountain on one ski, or any number of folks who have it so much worse than I do. I look at them and I know that nothing is impossible!

Life is full of challenges. How we handle them is a mark of maturity, and if we make the right choices, we gain respect not only from our peers, but from ourselves. So choose wisely. You have a long road ahead of you and I'm here to tell you, when you're an old guy like me, you're going to want to look back with pride on the journey!

Christopher E. Tubbs, Ph.D.

Christopher E. Tubbs, Ph.D.

Photo credit: Tubbs family

As the son of an NFL player and a television star, no one would have thought twice had Chris Tubbs opted to pursue a glamorous life in Hollywood. Instead, he decided to take the long, hard road to a Ph.D. . . . in *biochemistry*–a goal that is about as far removed from the glitter of Hollywood as one can get.

Chris pursued his undergraduate studies at North Carolina Central University (NCCU). While there, he took advantage of the opportunity to spend his junior year studying abroad at the Sorbonne University in Paris. A stand-out student, the United Negro College Fund (UNCF) awarded Chris a UNCF-Merck Undergraduate Fellowship covering 100 percent of his tuition costs for his junior and senior years.

He graduated cum laude from NCCU, and from there, he went on to pursue his Ph.D. at North Carolina State University (NCSU). Again, his stellar academic performance earned him funding in the form of a UNCF-Merck Graduate Science Research Dissertation Fellowship, as well as additional funding from the GEM Consortium, a competitive organization whose awards are reserved for highly qualified students pursuing graduate studies in engineering or science. The day Chris received his diploma, he had the added distinction of being one of the first African-Americans in NCSU's history to earn a Ph.D. in biochemistry.

Following his graduation from NCSU, Chris embarked on his postdoctoral work at the University of Minnesota's Department of Genetics, Cell Biology and Development. Yet again, he was awarded a UNCF-Merck Fellowship, this time from the UNCF-Merck Science Initiative. At the conclusion of his postdoctoral fellowship, Chris accepted an offer from Procter & Gamble pharmaceuticals to work in their Drug Discovery Research Division. Within three years, he was promoted to the position of senior medical science liaison, working on a national scale with physicians, health care professionals and other research entities.

Chris was a nominee for the prestigious Royan International Research Award in 2003. He holds a patent on a Method for Effecting Angiogenesis,* and is the author of numerous peer-reviewed journal articles. He is also a member of the planning advisory committee for the Center for Biotechnology and Biomedical Sciences at Norfolk State University.

Chris currently works at Vertex Pharmaceuticals as a medical science liaison in Hepatitis C research. He is also founder and senior partner of T-Squared Global Inc., a real estate investing company that serves the housing needs of the greater Houston marketplace.

---

*The full title of the patent is: Method of Effecting Angiogenesis by Modulating the Function of a Novel Endothelial.

Editor's Note

Chris Tubbs and I conducted this interview by telephone. Normally, I try to avoid telephone interviews because, unless you get lucky and connect right off the bat with your interviewee, it can be painfully difficult to develop any kind of rapport. You simply don't have the kind of information you need–facial expressions or body language, for example –to help steer the interview in the right direction. Well, I got lucky with Chris. Despite the sometimes serious nature of our discussion, I think we spent more time laughing than we did talking, and our scheduled 30-minute interview ended up lasting almost two hours.

As we talked, I realized that I had made an assumption about Chris that was incorrect. I assumed that because his father had played in the NFL and his mother and stepfather were on TV, life had been easy for him. I was certain he had been privy to an opulent, Hollywood lifestyle, but that was not the case. In fact, there were parts of Chris' life that were very tough, and he talks about those here. He also puts them into a larger context, showing how each challenge provided him with information about himself–information that ultimately allowed him to realize his dreams.

I am delighted to introduce Christopher E. Tubbs, Ph.D., the nicest guy I've never met.

A Conversation with Christopher E. Tubbs, Ph.D.

KHJ: What is one of the most powerful pieces of wisdom you have ever received?

Dr. Tubbs: One of the most powerful pieces of wisdom I've ever received came from my grandfather. When I was a kid, my grandfather would always tell me, "Be good to yourself." It is a sublime bit of wisdom, which, of course, went right over my head when I was young! I had no idea what it meant or how big a statement it was! In fact, it wasn't until I got into my late teens and early adulthood that it started to make sense to me. And now, as an adult, it has a *profound* impact on me and on how I live my life every day.

KHJ: When he said, "Be good to yourself," do you think he was telling you to pursue the things that make you happy?

Dr. Tubbs: I wouldn't put it quite that way. It's really, I think, about being genuine and making choices in life that reflect who you really are or who you hope to be.

KHJ: Can you give me an example of a time you put that into action and made that kind of choice?

Dr. Tubbs: I can give you an example of a time when I didn't! It happened when I was 14 or 15 years old and it still stands out as a turning point for me in my life. I was living in Chicago with my father at the time. He was working third shift, which is basically the night shift, and, consequently, I was by myself for long periods of time. There were elements of the "street" around where we lived–gang bangers, drug dealers, you name it. And, even though I hung out with some tough kids, I wasn't into those things. I didn't take advantage of those negative opportunities, so to speak.

But there was one time when I was hanging out with this guy who was maybe two years older than me. He pulled out a joint, started smoking it and then offered it to me. I told him, "No." I had never done anything like that nor had I ever felt the need to do anything like that. Plus, to be honest, I was scared. I didn't want to admit that, but I had seen what drugs could do to people and I was afraid of that happening to me. But he kept asking and, eventually, I caved in because I didn't want to seem like a punk. I took the joint and just kind of puffed on it. It tasted awful to me! And that was all I needed to say, "Oh man, I do *not* like this!" But in that moment, I knew I had betrayed myself. I had gone against who I was and done something I knew I didn't want to do, simply to please this guy.

I felt a tremendous amount of guilt afterwards. I kept asking myself why I'd done it. Why was this guy important enough to me for me to do something like that—something I didn't want to do? Nothing I came up with made me feel any better. The bottom line was that I had compromised my principles and it felt terrible.

KHJ: Did you have the opportunity to put what you had learned into practice as you got older? Maybe a time where you were able to say, "I'm not going to make that mistake again"?

Dr. Tubbs: Many times. The one that comes to mind, though, happened in high school. I went to a massive high school of 5,000 or more people. There was a lot of fighting that went on between the different ethnic groups: Puerto Ricans versus the blacks or blacks versus the Asians, or what have you.

I remember one time when a fight broke out between the blacks and the Puerto Ricans. This huge, mob-sized fight had started because one guy had said something to someone's girlfriend and the girlfriend got upset. The two guys started fighting and, the next thing you know, half of the school has joined in.

So there I am in the middle of this fight—and when I say "fight," I'm talking about serious fighting, with chains and knives and God knows what—and for whatever reason, I just stopped. I found myself standing in the mob of a hundred or more guys thinking, "*Why* am I here?" It all suddenly seemed so ridiculous. I knew my buddies were in there fighting and they expected me to be in there with them; but something inside me just said, "I am not going to participate in this." I didn't want to do it and I didn't want the consequences.

The next day I came to school to find out that there were guys in the hospital with their heads cracked open, with skull fractures, broken arms, crushed eye sockets. I felt terrible for the guys, but I knew, right then and there, that my decision had been the right one. I had figured out that I didn't want to be part of that fight and I had acted on that.

KHJ: It sounds like once you made the decision, though, it was pretty easy to follow through and walk away.

Dr. Tubbs: Yes and no. It was easy because I was older and had more practice at speaking up for myself. Like anything else, the more you do it, the easier it becomes. I think, too, what helped me that day was the level of violence and the fact that the fight was over something so petty. But even as I stepped out of the fight, I knew then there would be serious [social] consequences. My buddies were still fighting and I was standing on the outside. There are consequences to that. There are expectations, loyalties and obligations. And they're not unspoken. Afterwards, they confronted me and asked me what I thought I was doing and why I'd left. Their thought was, "We've had your back when you had things going on and we expected you to be there."

And that was true, and it had always been my intention to be there for them. But when it came to that fight, I never once regretted my decision on that field. I saw clearly that they had jumped into a fight that wasn't theirs. And standing up for myself became much easier after that, even though it was still scary at times.

I'll give you another example. I remember in college the football players would come into the cafeteria, walk right to the front of the line and step in front of whoever was there. They were big guys so no one wanted to stand up to them. But I got fed up with it, and one day I saw the big center on the football team standing in line and I stepped in front of him! Things got very tense and quiet right then. He got right up in my face and made some threats, but I stood my ground. At that moment I remembered my father. I felt as though he was standing there beside me telling me, "You make a decision and you stick with it. You know why you're doing what you're doing. And if you gotta go down, you go down. But you don't back down from what's right." So I stayed where I was, eye to eye with him and eventually he backed off. I put myself at risk that day but it was worth it to me because I was standing up for what I believed was right. And I had no problem with those guys after that.

I tell these stories because I think that the ability to stand up for yourself in the face of risk is an absolute necessity. As a grown man, you need to have that kind of self-confidence. Certainly, you need to be aware of your limitations. For example, I wasn't going to take on the center of the football team in a physical fight. But you must have a clear understanding within yourself of what you will or won't accept in terms of people's treatment of you or others. You will be tested at various points throughout your life, and if you don't have the confidence to know you can get through those tests, you won't reach your goals, whatever they may be. It's hard to do at first–to stand alone, apart from your peers–but over time you will build up that confidence that I think you need to be a man in the truest sense.

KHJ: I think it's interesting that both of the stories you tell were, or had the potential to be, violent situations. And yet, both times you took strong action that wasn't violent.

Dr. Tubbs: That's true. I think that's because what I'm talking about isn't physical intimidation as much as internal steel. I know from experience that if you're spending time on the streets, your physicality and your ability to hold your own is important. That's true. But the goal is not, or should not be, to stay on the streets. Your goal should be to progress out of that and into some kind of life that can sustain you. Violence narrows your choices in life and doors start shutting on you very quickly when you engage in that kind of behavior. Obviously, we're putting aside here situations that do call for that kind of action. If you see a child getting hurt, certainly I say get in and do whatever you need to do to protect that child from harm. Or if someone attacks you, you react in self-defense.

When I talk to young people, I tell them, "Write down your dreams on a piece of paper and put it somewhere–in your pocket or glove compartment, wherever. Then take it out and look at it from time to time. Especially when those tough decisions in life come up, you take that paper out and ask yourself, 'How is the decision I'm about to make going to affect me achieving this dream?'"

It always comes back to choices, and being good to yourself *through* those choices.

KHJ: What is one of the greatest personal challenges you have known?

Dr. Tubbs: My greatest challenge begins with my dream as a young man to earn my Ph.D. I wanted to be "Dr. Chris Tubbs." One of the many things my mother taught me was to always believe in my dreams. That said, she also let me know that we have to work for the things we want in life–dreams don't come true all by themselves. So, I knew it would require a lot of work to get to where I wanted to be. But I had no idea how much work and what kinds of obstacles I would run into.

I applied to graduate school at North Carolina State University and, initially, was told that I had not been accepted for the Ph.D. program because my test scores were too low. I had a mentor at the university who had encouraged me to apply there and, ultimately, through his intercession, I was accepted. I was the only black student in this particular Ph.D. program and my mentor warned me that I could expect the road to be difficult. My experience bore him out.

My first red flag came after I was in the program when I learned two white students, whose test scores were even lower than mine, had been accepted without question. So, where I was told that these test scores were a good indicator of my ability to succeed in this field, they had been told that the university didn't feel these test scores were indicative of their potential. In other words, they had been given the benefit of the doubt whereas I was told "You're just not smart enough." During the years I was there I was excluded from study groups, my questions were often rebuffed by professors, and nothing I did ever seemed to measure up in the eyes of my peers. It was a hard, lonely road and it made me question whether I was where I *wanted* to be or *should* be. I started to internalize what was happening and to question my ability.

I was lucky because my mentor was there to step in with encouragement and with a reality check, reminding me that I was smart and capable. And so I kept at it. But my years at N.C. State were some of the most difficult in my life and there were many, many times when I could not see the light at the end of the tunnel. I was sick and tired of being sick and tired, and I literally had to will myself to believe that I could make it. And I did. I became Dr. Chris Tubbs. I believe I also had the honor of becoming one of the first black persons at N.C. State to earn a Ph.D. in biochemistry. But the real value ended up being the *journey* I took to become Dr. Tubbs and the strength that the journey brought to my life.

There are some really difficult things you're going to have to get through in life. When you're in the midst of a struggle, you can so easily forget why you're struggling. All you know is that you want to stop struggling and to stop hurting. These are critical points that can make all the difference because you have to reach down farther than you knew you could go. But if you can go down into the pit and come back up and realize your goal, if you can see your way through to the end, you will walk away with an incredible sense of inner strength that you will carry with you for the rest of your life.

KHJ: I'm going switch gears for a moment and ask you to tell me about a living celebrity whom you admire and consider to be a role model.

Dr. Tubbs: I would say both my stepfather, Tim Reid, and my mother, Daphne Maxwell Reid. My stepfather, Tim, has been a huge influence in my life. I went to live with him and my mom when I was 16 years old. Up until then, I had lived with my dad during the school year and visited my mom and Tim during the summers. In the beginning, I actively fought against having any kind of relationship with him. My dad was going through a rough time and that was hard for me. Like any child of divorce, I didn't want anyone trying to step in and replace my dad. I was angry at my mom for leaving. And still, Tim kept reaching out to me. Though I was too proud at the time to let him know, I listened to what he said because he was giving me advice and wisdom that I needed, and I hadn't had a lot of men to look to when I was young who were successful and who took the time to talk with me. He taught me practical things–about saving and spending, for example. But he also taught me how to always think ahead and prepare myself for what's going to come later on down the road in life. We're very close now and I am grateful every day for him being in my life.

My mother is also someone I consider one of my life's greatest teachers. She is the calm in any storm. She gave me emotional strength and taught me compassion, patience and the importance of loving and respecting women. She truly flows with life's energy, through both the ups and the downs. Her philosophy is, "It will be what it is, so enjoy the ride." I refer back to her example and her advice often.

KHJ: Wonderful. Now for some word association. Bullies.

Dr. Tubbs: Hate 'em.

KHJ: Boys don't cry.

Dr. Tubbs: Bullshit.

KHJ: Compassion.

Dr. Tubbs: Essential.

KHJ: Respect for women.

Dr. Tubbs: The route to love.

How to Order Additional Copies of
A Better Man

Do you know a group that might be interested in this book? Perhaps you're affiliated with a school, a church, an association, or a business whose members would appreciate the message of *A Better Man*.

Charitable organizations, in particular, are often in a unique position to reach those who can benefit from its lessons. The editor and Brandylane Publishers Inc. are committed to supporting charitable organizations in their efforts to assist those in need. Please contact us directly for volume discount options.

A Better Man can be a great fundraiser as well! By purchasing the book in bulk and selling it at a premium to supporters—either "as is" or customized for your organization*—you can earn money for a worthy cause while sharing a very worthwhile message.

Place Your Order:

Online: www.abettermanbook.com or
www.brandylanepublishers.com

By phone: (804) 644-3090

By e-mail: community@abettermanbook.com or
rhpruett@brandylanepublishers.com

*Customized Edition: To maximize the appeal of *A Better Man* to your supporters, Brandylane Publishers Inc. can customize the book for your organization. It can create a special edition of the book with your logo on the cover and an additional page in the interior reserved for your personal letter to the readers and/or other information about your services. (Minimum purchase required. Please contact us for details.)